The Commentary of Abraham ibn Ezra on the Pentateuch

Volume 3: Leviticus

translated by

Jay F. Shachter

Ktav Publishing House

Hoboken NJ

5746 / 1986

The Straightforward Meaning
[*Sefer Hayyashar*]
by Abraham the Poet
Firmly Rooted in the Intricacies of Grammar
May It Serve The Cause of Correct Understanding
and May It Gladden All Who Use It

O my God, the God of my sire Abraham,
Grant kindness to me, to Your slave ABRAHAM.
May the words of Your wisdom be taught to the ear
Of Your servant, THE SON OF Your servant ME'IR.
And may Your salvation come down from afar
To the person whose title is IBN 'EZRA.

Dedication

To
Dr and Mrs Offenbacher,
Dr and Mrs Gribetz,
Mr and Mrs Leibler,
Judge and Mrs Kleiman,
and
Mrs Weiss

Acknowledgments

The guidance provided by Rabbi Abraham Lipshitz has greatly improved the quality of this translation. The library and the human resources of Yeshivas Brisk have supplied references for many of ibn Ezra's allusions and have clarified some difficult passages. The English translation of Pentateuchal passages was influenced by Rabbi Charles Kahane's *Torah Yesharah.* The *Meḥoqeqey Yehuda* of the late Rabbi Yehuda Krinsky served as primary commentary on the text, supplemented by the commentary of the late Rabbi Shlomo Zalman Netter.

My greatest debt, however, is to Abraham ibn Ezra himself, and to his teachers and their teachers before them, who preserved and clarified traditions dating back to Moses, and gave them over to the keeping of future generations.

The Translator

Library of Congress Cataloging-in-Publication Data

Ibn Ezra, Abraham ben Meïr, 1092–1167.
The commentary of Abraham Ibn Ezra on the Pentateuch.

Translation of: Perush ha-Torah.
Includes index.
Contents: — v. 3. Leviticus.
1. Bible. O. T. Pentateuch—Commentaries.
I. Shachter, Jay F. II. Title.
BS1225.I3213 1986 222′.107 86-20991
ISBN 0-88125-109-7 (v. 3)

Manufactured in the United States of America

A Point of Law

Jewish law forbids one to accept payment for teaching Torah. Yet this book is not being given away — it is being sold. One must not conclude from the behavior of the publisher, however, that an individual is permitted to draw a salary for teaching. Several factors combine which possibly render the sale of this book permissible:

1) The cost of printing books is not directly proportional to the number of books printed. Publishing entails both fixed costs and variable costs. Certain initial expenses — e.g., setting up the plates — must occur no matter how many copies are made. Other expenses — e.g., buying paper — depend on the size of the printing. Thus, unless you can predict exactly how many copies you will sell, it is impossible to establish a selling price that guarantees neither a profit nor a loss. Consequently, a sufficiently popular book will necessarily make money, while a sufficiently unpopular book will necessarily lose money, and there is no way to avoid both possibilities simultaneously.
2) The prohibition against teaching Torah professionally extends only to the oral Torah (*tora sheb'al peh*). One is permitted to collect a fee for teaching the written Torah (*tora shebikhtav*). Although this book contains *tora sheb'al peh*, it also contains *tora shebikhtav*; the portions of the book which may be sold are inseparable from the portions of the book which may not be sold.
3) The author of the book has been dead for several centuries and will collect no earthly royalties from it. The only people collecting royalties will be the publisher and the translator. Translating someone else's teachings is not the same thing as teaching something yourself, therefore it may be forbidden to do the latter, but not the former, for money. (This reason is probably the weakest of the four. Every translation is perforce an interpretation. Ibn Ezra himself often called the early Sages the *ma'atiqim.*)
4) A book is a physical commodity. Conceivably, giving a lecture falls under the definition of "teaching", but selling a commodity does not fall under that definition.

The absence of any of these four factors would have rendered the sale of this book of questionable legality. In fact, the legality of the sale ought still to be considered questionable. I do not hereby supply a *psaq din*, and no one should derive a *hetter* for similar behavior either from my actions or from their defense.

It should go without saying — but perhaps it must be said — that these words must not serve as a pretext for criticising the well-intentioned actions of any other human being. Observing *Hilkhot Talmud Tora*, 1:7, does not allow one to disregard *Hilkhot De'ot*, 2:3. Whoever uses the above point of law to justify feelings of disrespect or disdain commits a crime far more serious than any which I have here tried to prevent.

The Translator

Table of Contents

[1:1]GOD called to Moshe and spoke to him from within the Tent of Assembly, saying: [2]Speak to the Children of Israel and say to them: "Any man who brings, from among you, a sacrifice to GOD — you will bring your offering

---

[1:1] Just as the covenant of circumcision serves two distinct purposes [Genesis 17:1; Genesis 17:11], so it is possible for a single commandment to serve many different purposes — like the commandments of the burnt-offering and other sacrifices:

1) In offering up the appropriate portion at the appropriate time, we who have a portion in the world to come are apportioned proportionately. Thus the word "to atone" literally means "to ransom" (this is evidenced in the beginning of the *parasha* of *Ki Tis̀sa* [Exodus 30:12], and it explains the phrase "lest he strike us with pestilence" [Exodus 5:3]).
2) The burnt offerings also contain profound allusions to natural history.
3) By studying each sacrifice, one may come fundamentally to understand the nature of sin, and the nature of our obligations to sustain the teachers of the Torah.

GOD called to Moshe Since Scripture has already stated that "Moshe was not allowed..." [Exodus 40:35], GOD must have called him from within the Tent of Assembly, telling him to enter therein, where He would speak to him. Moshe used to go behind the Partition, where the Glory resided (for so it is written [Exodus 25:22]).[1] The reason for mentioning the sacrifices before the other commandments is that the Divine Presence would depart if they did not keep the law of the daily burnt-offering (which eventually happened). Perish the thought that GOD should *need* a burnt-offering! As it is written: "If I were hungry, I would not tell you" [Psalms 50:12]. The subject is admittedly too profound to explain easily. **[2] from among you**:

- This word appears later in the sentence than is syntactically called for. The sentence is understood as if it read, "any man *among you* who brings a sacrifice...". Many Hebrew sentences exhibit similar constructions.

---

[1]This is the meaning of "He beholds the form of GOD" [Numbers 12:8].

from domestic stock: from cattle, or from the flock. [3]If he brings a burnt-offering from the cattle, he will bring an unblemished male to the entrance of the Tent of Assembly. He will bring it willingly before GOD. [4]He will place his hand on the burnt offering's head, and it will be

---

or

- Scripture employs synecdoche and connotes "from your possessions" by the words "from you".

or

- By altering its location in the sentence, and stressing "from *you*", Scripture alludes to the unacceptability of bringing offerings of stolen animals. Compare, "I hate robbery with burnt offerings" [Isaiah 61:8].

from domestic stock The sacrifice must be from this general category. Scripture then specifies **from cattle**, and **from the flock** — itself a category that includes the two species of sheep and goats. **your offering** This word is also a general category. **[3] a burnt-offering** This is one category of sacrifice; and its name is self-explanatory [*comment on* 6:1]. **from the cattle** Either a fully grown or a young animal may be offered, so long as it is at least eight days old. Since the entire burnt offering is offered to the Most High, a choice animal must be used. Therefore, females are not used for burnt offerings, because male animals are preferable to female animals. **unblemished** without defects. After having said **he will bring**, Scripture goes on to specify *where* he shall bring it, once he has entered the Courtyard of the Tent of Assembly. **before GOD** This phrase is a displaced continuation of the clause, **he will bring it to the entrance of the Tent of Assembly**. The word **willingly** indicates that he must offer the sacrifice voluntarily, and not out of obligation. **[4] He will place his hand** [*singular*] It seems from a literal interpretation of the verse that he places a single hand (for we cannot assume that the scapegoat [16:21] resembles the other offerings, insofar as there Scripture specifically mentions how many hands are to be placed). However, the Exegetes, upon whom we rely, have determined that all laying on of hands involves both hands [Yoma 36a]. ¶The animal which atones for an emergent impulse is called a **burnt offering** [literally: an arising]. Similarly, the animals brought to atone for sin and guilt are called sin-

accepted, to atone for him. [5]He will slaughter the ox before GOD, and the sons of Aaron, the kohanim, will bring the blood, and will throw the blood around the sides of the altar at the entrance of the Tent of Assembly. [6]He will skin the burnt-offering and carve it into its limbs. [7]The sons of Aaron the kohen will light a fire on the altar, and arrange wood on the fire. [8]The sons of Aaron, the kohanim, will arrange the limbs, the head, and the fats upon the wood of the fire on the altar. [9]He will wash its innards and its legs with water, and the kohen will kindle all on the altar for a burnt-offering, consumed by fire, that

---

offerings and guilt-offerings, respectively. **it will be accepted** he will obtain GOD's good will **to atone for him** to release him from the punishment due him **[5] before GOD** The same phrase is used apropos the sheep burnt offering [:11], where the subsequent phrase "the northern side of the Altar" localizes the slaughter directly opposite the Table. One kohen **will slaughter** [*singular*] the animal, but many **will throw** [*plural*] **the blood**, as it is written: "Aaron's sons handed him the blood" [9:12]. **the one at the entrance of the Tent** i.e., *not* the Incense Altar **[6] He will skin** either a kohen, or the Levite attached to his service **[7] The sons of Aaron** for the Levites may not approach the Altar. This commandment falls upon **[8] kohanim** — the use of the plural means that no fewer than two must participate. **the fats** Many contemporary scholars have understood this word to mean "the carcass". In my opinion, the word denotes suet. Thus: **The sons of Aaron, the kohanim, will arrange the limbs** — the pieces of the body; **[and] the head, and the fats** — i.e., the suet.[1] Also: "He will carve it into its limbs" [:12] — and these limbs of the carcass include "its head and its fats" [:12] (or, perhaps, the phrase means "*with* its head and its fats", following common Hebrew idiom — but conclusive evidence to the contrary appears in "Moshe kindled the head, and the pieces, and the fats" [8:20]) **[9] will wash with water** This is done either by a kohen or by a Levite. Thus Scripture must specify that **the kohen**

---

[1]Scripture omits the word "and", in accordance with Hebrew usage (compare, "a ruby, [and] a topaz, and a rock-crystal" [Exodus 28:17]).

is willingly accepted by GOD.

[10] If his burnt-offering is from the flock, whether of sheep or of goats, he will offer an unblemished male. [11] He will slaughter it at the northern side of the altar, before GOD, and the sons of Aaron, the kohanim, will throw its blood around the sides of the altar. [12] He will carve it into its limbs, which the kohen will arrange with its head and fats on the wood of the fire on the altar. [13] He will wash the innards and the legs with water, and the kohen will bring and kindle all on the altar; it is a burnt-offering consumed by fire that is willingly accepted by GOD.

[14] If his burnt-offering to GOD is of fowl, he will bring his offering from turtledoves, or from the young of pigeons. [15] The kohen will bring it to the altar, and behead it, and kindle it on the altar. Its blood will be squeezed out against the wall of the altar. [16] He will remove its crop with its outer feathers, and cast it beside the altar, to the

---

is the one who **will kindle**. The word **burnt-offering** is an adjective, denoting an offering involving fire, and it modifies the word **all**. **willingly accepted** previously explained [*comment on* Exodus 29:25]

[11] at the northern side but not actually adjoining (as in, "on the northern side" [Psalms 48:3]. They are mistaken who say that the Tower of Zion was inside Jerusalem)

[14] turtledoves fully grown, not young ones. **young of pigeons** Scripture does not simply say "pigeons", to exclude the fully-grown **[15] behead** This word has no cognate: the form of beheading is known only from tradition. **its blood will be squeezed out** a verb in the *nif'al* form, from "you have drained" [Isaiah 51:17] **[16] its crop** The meaning of this word is known, and it is related to "Woe to the filthy" [Zephaniah 3:1] **with its** [the crop's]

east, toward the ash-heap. [17] He will split it by its wings, but will not divide it completely; the kohen will kindle it on the altar, on the wood of the fire. It is a burnt-offering consumed by fire, willingly accepted by GOD.

[2:1] If someone should offer a cereal-offering to GOD, his offering will be of fine flour; he will pour oil over it, and put frankincense upon it. [2] He will bring it to Aaron's sons, the kohanim. He shall scoop out a fistful from its fine flour and oil, besides all its frankincense; the kohen will kindle its memorial-part on the altar: an offering consumed by fire, willingly accepted by GOD. [3] What remains of the cereal-offering will be for Aaron and his sons, most

---

outer feathers i.e., with the bird's outer feathers (as in, "full of feathers" [Ezekiel 17:3]) **beside the Altar** here the word means "outside the Altar" **to the east** far away from the holy place **toward the ash-heap** not just toward the ash-heap, but actually on it **[17] He will split** as in "completely cleft" [11:3], meaning "cut"

[2:1] If someone [literally: if a soul] **should offer** i.e., the soul of a man. Scripture mentions the word "soul" because the cereal-offering that is described here is a freewill offering; and the word "soul" is often used to denote voluntary donations (e.g., "uphold me with a generous spirit" [Psalms 51:14]). **fine-flour** well-ground wheat flour (*sameed* in Arabic). It is unfitting for anything to be offered to the Most High that is not of the highest quality. **[2] He shall scoop out a fistful** from "storehouses" [Genesis 41:47] (our ancestors, whose words are true, have explained [Yoma 47a] the manner and form of a **fistful**) **from its fine flour** i.e., a small part of it. Likewise, a small part of the oil is taken. However, the kohen kindles **all of its frankincense**. The *'alef* in **its memorial-part** [Hebrew: *'azkaratah*] is superfluous. The word denotes that which serves to remind one of GOD, for Whose sake the meal-offering is brought. Other people interpret the word as a reference to the odor of incense [e.g., Genesis 8:21] (compare, "his fragrance shall be like the wine of Lebanon" [Hosea 14:8]) **[3] for Aaron and his**

holy among the fire-offerings to GOD.

[4]If you bring a cereal-offering baked in the oven, bring either maṣṣa loaves of fine flour mixed with oil, or maṣṣa wafers smeared with oil.

[5]If your cereal-offering is fried in a pan, it will be maṣṣa of fine flour mixed with oil. [6]Crumble it into pieces and pour oil on it: it is a cereal-offering.

[7]If your offering is a braised cereal-offering, it will be made of fine flour with oil. [8]You will bring the cereal-offering made of these ingredients to GOD and present it to the kohen; he will bring it to the altar. [9]The kohen will lift out the memorial-part from the cereal-offering, and kindle it on the altar as an offering consumed by fire, willingly accepted by GOD. [10]What is left of the cereal-offering after the fire-offering will be most holy for Aaron and his sons. [11]Any cereal-offering you bring to GOD will not be leavened, for you must kindle no leaven, nor any

---

sons for all the kohanim equally

[4] loaves [Hebrew: *ḥallot*] i.e., solid maṣṣa. Some say they had to be round (from the Old Hebrew "rotation" [*ḥalila*] [e.g., Sukka 55b]).

[5] fried in a pan one plate underneath one plate. The *tav* interchanges with the *heh* (like the *tav* in "It shall return to the prince" [Hebrew: *veshavat*] [Ezekiel 46:17]).

[7] braised i.e., fried. Some people claim the word derives from "my heart overflows" [Psalms 45:2], on account of the noisiness of the process. **[10] for Aaron and his sons** i.e., his sons who will come after him (meaning, the officiating kohen — for so it is written regarding the two kinds of meal-offerings [7:9-10]) **[11]**

honey, as an offering to be consumed by fire for GOD.
[12]You may bring them to GOD as offerings of first-fruit, but they will not be willingly accepted to be burnt on the altar.
[13]You must season all your cereal-offerings with salt. You must not withhold the salt of your God's covenant from your cereal-offerings. You must bring salt with all your offerings.

[14]If you bring a first-fruit offering to GOD, bring ripe ears dried in fire, ground-grain and fresh-grain as the cereal-offering of your first-fruits.
[15]Put oil on it, and place frankincense on it, for it is a cereal-offering.
[16]The

---

leaven the agent that causes bread to rise **honey** also a leavening agent. Many people have said that the word **honey** here, and in every occurrence of "a land flowing with milk and honey" [e.g., Exodus 3:8], denotes honey made from dates. Grounds for their interpretation can be found in Ezra's book [II Chronicles 31:5]. **[12] You may bring them to GOD as offerings of first-fruit** This denotes the "two [loaves, each made] of two-tenths [of an *'efa*]," [23:17] which are waved before GOD on the holiday of Shavu'ot. Despite the fact that they are consecrated **to GOD**, they are to be eaten by the kohen. **[13] your God's covenant** I have made you party to a covenant, and I have bound you not to offer a worthless sacrifice. Nor may such a sacrifice be eaten: it would be disrespectful.

[14] If you bring a first-fruit offering Many people claim [*Mekhilta* on Exodus 20:22] that this is one case where the word "if" introduces an unconditional clause. In my opinion, there is no need for such an assertion. Only the bringing of the *choicest* first fruit is obligatory [Exodus 23:19], not ordinary first fruits. Anyone who wishes, however, to bring a freewill offering of first fruits, may do so. **ripe ears** [Hebrew: *'aviv*] so called because it is the original form of the grain, from "progenitor" [Hebrew: *'av*] **ground-grain** The meaning of this word is known (compare, "my soul is consumed" [Psalms 119:20] even though there the cognate is spelled with a *samekh*, not a *śin*) **fresh-grain** as in, "...and full ears of corn

kohen will kindle its memorial-part, some ground-grain and some oil with all the frankincense, as an offering consumed by fire for GOD.

[3:1]If his offering is a peace-offering: If he offers it from cattle, he may offer an unblemished male or female before GOD. [2]He will place his hand on the head of his offering, and slaughter it at the entrance to the Tent of Assembly; Aaron's descendants, the kohanim, will throw the blood around the sides of the altar. [3]From the peace-offering he must bring a fire-offering to GOD: the fat that covers the stomach, all the fat that is on the stomach, [4]the two kidneys, and the fat on them – which is near the loins – and he will remove the lobe on top of the liver, with the kidneys. [5]Aaron's descendants will kindle it on the altar after the burnt-offering, on the wood of the fire: an offering consumed by fire, willingly accepted by GOD.

[6]If his peace-offering to GOD is of the flock he will offer an unblemished male or female. [7]If he brings a lamb for his offering, he will bring it before GOD. [8]He will place his hand on the head of his offerings, and slaughter it in front of the Tent of Assembly; and Aaron's sons will throw its blood around the sides of the altar. [9]From the peace-offering he will make a fire-offering to GOD. He will remove its suet [for want of a better term, the word

---

in his sack" [II Kings 4:42]

[3:1] peace-offering to be defined **[4] the loins** [Hebrew: *hakksalim*] The meaning of this word is known from the phrase "The stars of heaven and its constellations [Hebrew: *ukhsileyhem*]" [Isaiah 13:10]. **with the kidneys** [literally: on the kidneys] as in "the men came with the women" [literally: on the women] [Ex-

"suet" will be used to denote organic, as opposed to subcutaneous, fat — Translator]: the entire fat-tail, adjoining the spinal column; the fat that covers the stomach; all the fat on the stomach; [10]the two kidneys, and the fat on them — which is near the loins; and he will remove the lobe on top of the liver, with the kidneys. [11]The kohen will kindle it on the altar as food for the fire dedicated to GOD.

[12]If his offering is a goat, he will bring it before GOD.
[13]He will place his hand on its head, and slaughter it in front of the Tent of Assembly. Aaron's sons will throw its blood around the sides of the altar. [14]He will offer from it his fire-sacrifice to GOD: the fat that covers the stomach; all the fat on the stomach; [15]the two kidneys,

---

odus 35:22]

[9] its suet: the entire fat-tail This phrase is to be understood literally, for the fat-tail falls under the category of suet. Thus the Sadducees [a derogatory reference to Karaites — Translator] are in error, as I shall explain in the *parasha* of *Ṣav* [*comment on* 7:23]. Sa'adya Gaon also erred in saying that the verse should read, "its suet, and the fat tail...." This interpretation violates Hebrew usage; if it were correct, Scripture should either have said "*its* suet, and *its* fat-tail" or "*the* suet, and *the* fat-tail". **the spinal column** This word is understood from its context, since it has no cognate. Some people derive it from the word "wood", but that is far-fetched. **[11] food** [literally: bread] **for the fire** I have already explained that the word "bread" is often used in Hebrew to denote food in general [*comment on* Exodus 16:4]. It can refer to fruit [Jeremiah 11:19] as well as to flesh.

[12] If a goat [*feminine*] i.e., from the *species* of goat, whether male or female, like the sheep [:7]. Scripture does not mention the fat-tail here, or further on concerning cattle, since goats and cattle have negligible fat-tails. Moreover, the sheep native to Israel are

and the fat on them – which is near the loins; and he will remove the lobe on top of the liver, with the kidneys. [16]The kohen will kindle them on the altar as food for the fire, willingly accepted. All of this fat will be offered to GOD. [17]It is an everlasting decree for your generations in all your dwelling places: Eat no suet or blood."

[4:1]GOD told Moshe: [2]Tell the Children of Israel: "If anyone sins unintentionally against any of GOD's commandments, doing one of the things that should not be done: [3]If the Annointed Kohen commits a sin that brings the people to guilt, he must offer an unblemished bullock of the herd to GOD as a sin-offering to atone on his sin which he committed. [4]He will bring the bullock to the entrance

---

known to have very big fat-tails. [16] **all of this fat** [*singular*] used here as a collective noun [17] Now that the fats and the blood have been set apart for GOD, they are forbidden to you. **an everlasting decree** I shall explain this at length in the *parasha* of *Ṣav* [*comment on* 7:23]

[4:2] **if anyone sins** by mistakenly doing something that is prohibited, and punishable either by *karet* or by flogging **anyone** includes both the native born and the convert, as it is written [Numbers 15:15]. [3] Scripture now goes into the details, beginning with the High Priest (i.e., the kohen who is anointed). **that brings the people to guilt**

- He promulgated something that was incorrect, and the entire nation sinned unintentionally;

or

- By sinning, the High Priest inculpates every person. This expression is used because it is the High Priest who carries the burden of the Torah. He must be preserved free from sin, because he is personally consecrated to GOD.

to atone on his sin i.e., to atone *for* his sin. Since he is a great man, he must sacrifice a bullock, which is the greatest of the

of the Tent of Assembly before GOD. He will place his hand on the head of the bullock, and slaughter it before GOD. [5]The Annointed Kohen will take some of the bullock's blood and bring it into the Tent of Assembly. [6]The kohen will dip his finger in the blood, and will sprinkle of the blood seven times before GOD in front of the holy Partition. [7]The kohen will put some of the blood on the corners of the altar of fragrant incense, before GOD, in the Tent of Assembly. He will pour all of the bullock's blood at the base of the altar for burnt-offerings, which is at the entrance of the Tent of Assembly. [8]He will remove all the fat of the bullock sin-offering from it: the fat that covers the stomach; all the fat on the stomach; [9]the two kidneys, and the fat on them – which is near the loins; and he will remove the lobe on top of the liver, with the kidneys, [10]as was removed from the bull of the peace-offering. The kohen will kindle them on the altar for burnt-offerings. [11]But the skin of the bullock, all the flesh, including its head, its legs, its innards, and its dung – [12]he will take all of the bullock out of the camp to a ritually pure place where the ashes are poured out. He will burn it on wood with fire; it will be burned on the place where the ashes are to be poured.

[13]If the entire Assembly of Israel will err, and the public

---

offerings. [6] **The kohen will dip his finger** i.e., the High Priest. The significance of **seven times** is explained in the *parasha* of *Balaq* [*comment on* Numbers 23:1]. Because of the High Priest's great stature, the blood of his sin-offering is sprinkled **in front of the holy Partition**, and [7] on the corners of the Incense Altar. [8] Except for the organic fats, [11] all of the bullock [12] is to be burned *outside*, for it is not a burnt-offering. **where the ashes are to be poured** There must be ashes from the Altar in the place where

will be unaware of the error, and will do one of those things that GOD has commanded not to do, thereby incurring guilt: [14]When the sin, regarding which they have sinned, will be disclosed, the public will offer a bullock of the herd as a sin-offering and will bring it before the Tent of Assembly. [15]The elders of the assembly will place their hands on the bullock's head before GOD, and he will slaughter the bullock before GOD. [16]The Annointed Kohen will bring some of the blood into the Tent of Assembly. [17]The kohen will dip his finger in the blood, and will sprinkle seven times before GOD in front of the Partition. [18]He will put some of the blood on the corners of the altar that is before GOD inside the Tent of Assembly. He will pour out all the blood at the base of the altar for burnt-offerings, which is at the entrance of the Tent of Assembly. [19]He will remove all its suet from it, and kindle it on the altar. [20]He will do with the bullock exactly as he did with the bullock of the sin-offering; the kohen

---

it is burnt.

[14] When the sin will be disclosed This rule also applies to the High Priest: as long as he does not realize his sin, and as long as he is not informed, he does not bring the bullock sin-offering.[1] The reason why this rule — **When the sin becomes disclosed** — is mentioned first here, regarding the Sanhedrin, is that the High Priest is likely to inform them of their error, whereas no one is likely to inform the High Priest; he himself must become aware of *his* error. The sin-offering of the Assembly is identical in all details to the sin-offering of the High Priest. Thus, the High Priest is equal in stature to all Israel. **[15] The elders of the assembly** i.e., the leaders. They place their hands for themselves, and for all Israel, since it is impossible for every person in Israel to place

[1]There are those who say that the High Priest brings this sacrifice once a year, in case he sinned.

will make atonement for them, and they will be forgiven.
[21]He will take the bullock outside the camp, and burn it as he burned the aforementioned bullock; it is the public's sin-offering.

[22]If a chief sins unintentionally by doing any one of the things which GOD, his God, commanded not to be done, thereby incurring guilt: [23]When he becomes aware of the sin he has committed, he will bring an unblemished male

---

his hands himself. **[21] it is the public's sin-offering** i.e., the bullock. But if Israel should err, and *not* do one of the *positive* commandments, then they must bring a bullock burnt-offering and a male goat sin-offering [Numbers 15:24].

[22] If a chief sins The verb and noun are reversed, to mean "If he who sins is the chief...." This verse is a continuation of the previous paragraph, beginning, "If the entire Assembly of Israel" [:13], as if Scripture had said, "and if the sinner is a chief of a tribe, or of a clan," **[23] When he becomes aware** Scripture employs brevity, as in the case of the High Priest [:3]; but the intent is to include *both* the case when the chief learns himself that he has sinned, *and* the case when someone who observed him in the act informs him. The phrase **he becomes aware** employs a verb in the past tense (as in "when you are besieged" [Deuteronomy 28:52]). Scripture omits the actor, as in "who was born to Levi" [Numbers 26:59]. Rabbi Moshe ben Shmu'el Gikatilla HaKohen holds that the verb is in the passive voice, for the *ḥolem* vowel interchanges with the *shuruq* vowel (as in, "Joseph had been brought down to Egypt" [Genesis 39:1]). The chief brings a male goat, as Sa'adya Gaon pointed out when he explained the verse, "a greyhound, and a male goat," [Proverbs 30:31] in his commentary on the Book of Proverbs. Although the animal is male, because of the chief's high stature, nevertheless:

1) Its blood is not brought into the Sanctuary; and
2) The kohanim eat from the chief's sin-offering, to secure atonement for him, as it is written [:27]; even though the High Priest does not eat from his own sin-

goat as his offering. [24] He will place his hand on the goat's head, and he will slaughter it at the place where the burnt-offering is slaughtered, before GOD; it is a sin-offering. [25]The kohen will take some of the sin-offering's blood with his finger, and smear it on the corners of the altar for burnt-offerings. He will pour its blood at the base of the altar for burnt-offerings. [26]He will kindle all its suet on the altar, as with the suet of the peace-offering. The kohen will secure atonement for his sin, and he will be forgiven.

[27]If any ordinary person sins unintentionally by doing one of the things that GOD commanded not to be done, and thereby committed an offense: [28]When he becomes aware of the sin he has committed, he will bring an unblemished female goat as his offering for the sin he committed. [29]He will place his hand on the head of the sin-offering, and will slaughter the sin-offering at the burnt-offering place. [30]The kohen will take some of its blood on his finger, and smear it on the corners of the altar for burnt-offerings. He will pour all its blood at the base of the altar. [31]He will remove all its suet, as the suet was removed from the peace-offering, and the kohen will kindle it on the altar as an offering willingly accepted by GOD. The kohen will secure atonement for him, and he will be forgiven.

---

offering.

[27] an ordinary person denotes all Israelites, all ordinary kohanim, and all Levites. **committed an offense** a verb in the past tense, like "Isaac was old" [Genesis 27:1] **[28] a female goat** because his stature is less than that of the chief **[31] he will be forgiven** This concept is explained in the *parasha* of *Shlaḥ Lkha* [*com-*

[32] If he bring a sheep as his offering for a sin-offering, he will bring an unblemished female. [33]He will place his hand on the head of the sin-offering, and he will slaughter it as a sin-offering at the place where the burnt-offering is slaughtered. [34]The kohen will take some of the sin-offering's blood with his finger and smear it on the corners of the altar for burnt-offerings. He will pour all its blood at the base of the altar. [35]He will remove all its suet, as the suet of the lamb peace-offering was removed, and the kohen will kindle it on the altar with GOD's offerings that are consumed by fire. The kohen will secure atonement for the sin he committed, and he will be forgiven.

[5:1]Anyone who sins, having heard admission of guilt, if he was a witness (whether he saw, or he knew), and if he does not tell, he has committed an offense; [2]or anyone who touches any ritually impure thing, either the carcass of a ritually impure wild animal, or the carcass of a ritually impure domesticated beast, or the carcass of a ritually impure creeping being, and is unaware of it, and com-

---

ment on Numbers 14:19]. **[32] if he bring a sheep** [*masculine*] that is, if he bring from the *species* [*masculine*] of sheep, then he should bring a female, like the female goat [:28] **[35] as the suet of the lamb peace-offering was removed** to include the fat-tail, since the female goat does not have a fat-tail

[5:1] anyone who sins, having heard admission of guilt specifically, regarding forbidden articles (as in, "you admitted your guilt" [Judges 17:2]). Although Scripture employs brevity, it implicitly warns the witness that he is obliged to testify, since if he does *not* testify, he is subject to Divine punishment: **he has committed an offense**. This applies when the witness forgot to testify, and afterward remembered. **[2] or anyone who touches any ritually impure thing** This denotes the carcass of one of the four enumerated

mits an offense while ritually impure; [3] or if he touches a human ritual impurity, or any impurity — whatever has caused him to become ritually impure — and he is unaware of it, and then discovers that he has committed an offense; [4] or if anyone swears, pronouncing with his lips, to do harm, or to do good, concerning anything regarding which one may utter an oath, and he then forgets, and then becomes aware that he has committed an offense: In any of these cases, [5] when he becomes guilty, in any of these cases, he will confess his sin, [6] and he will bring his guilt-offering to GOD for the sin he committed: a female from the flock, either a lamb or a goat, as a sin-offering. The kohen will make atonement for his sin. [7] If he cannot afford a lamb, he will bring as his guilt-offering for his sin two turtle-doves or two young pigeons to GOD:

---

beasts (the swine and its fellows) [11:4–7]. **or the carcass of a ritually impure beast** i.e., ritually impure as food, like the horse or the donkey **a ritually impure creeping being** one of the eight enumerated [11:29–30] **he was unaware of it** and afterward found out. This applies also **[3]** to someone who touches a man who suffers from a constant flow, someone who touches someone else who had contact with a corpse, someone who touches a woman who suffers from a constant flow, and someone who touches a menstruant. **[4] pronouncing with his lips** i.e., spoken out loud **to do harm** to someone who is guilty toward him (or, according to Sa'adya Gaon, to harm *himself*). The reason Scripture mentions **in any of these cases** here is that these sins must be confessed; but **[5]** the other sins that Scripture mentions are negative commandments, and do not require confession before the kohen [but they do require confession before God — Translator]. In either case, the sacrifice is the same. **[7] if he cannot afford** [literally: if his arm cannot reach] Since it is with one's arm that one generally labors, and it is the arm that acquires objects, Scripture uses this metaphor to allude to one who lacks something. **one as a sin-offering and one as a burnt-offering** Rabbi Yiṣḥaq said that the rea-

one as a sin-offering and the other as a burnt-offering.
[8]He will bring them to the kohen, who will offer the one brought as a sin-offering first. He will cut off its head at the back of the neck, but he will not divide it.
[9]He will squirt some of the blood of the sin-offering on the wall of the altar, and the remaining blood will be squeezed out at the base of the altar; it is a sin-offering.
[10]He will make the second a standard burnt-offering. The kohen will secure atonement for him for the sin he committed, and he will be forgiven.

[11]If he cannot afford two turtle-doves, or two young pigeons, the offering he brings for the sin committed shall be one-tenth of an *'efa* of fine flour, for a sin-offering. He will put no oil in it, nor will he put any frankincense on it, for it is a sin-offering.
[12] He will bring it to the kohen. The kohen will scoop out a fistful as its memorial-part, and burn it on the altar, upon the fire-offerings of GOD. It is a sin-offering.
[13]The kohen will secure atonement for him for the sin he committed in any of the above cases, and he will be forgiven. It belongs to the kohen, like any cereal-offering."

[14]GOD told Moshe:
[15]If any person commits an offense, and sins unintentionally concerning the things consecrated to GOD, he will bring his guilt-offering to GOD: an unblemished ram from the flock, worth silver shekels (of the

---

son for the burnt-offering is that, since he could not afford a lamb, perhaps an evil thought entered his head. The more straightforward explanation, in my opinion, is: One provides the equivalent of the fats of a sin-offering that are wholly consumed, while the other is the actual sin-offering that is called for by law.

holy shekels), for a guilt-offering. [16]He will repay what he desecrated from the consecrated objects, adding a fifth to it, and will give that to the kohen. The kohen will make atonement for him with the guilt-offering ram, and he will be forgiven.

[17]If someone should sin by doing any one of the things which GOD has commanded not to be done — but he does not know whether he transgressed — he has committed an offense. [18]He will bring an unblemished ram from the flock, whose value is that of a guilt-offering, to the kohen. The kohen will make atonement for him for the error which he does not know that he committed, and he will be forgiven. [19]It is a guilt-offering. He has incurred guilt

---

[11] **one-tenth of an *'efa*** food for one man for one day

[15] **an offense** [Hebrew: *ma'al*] something that was concealed from him (from the word "covering" [Hebrew: *m'il*]), here denoting a desecration of the articles consecrated to GOD. He must bring a ram that is worth **shekels** — the use of the plural means at least two shekels. [16] In the case when he originally sinned unknowingly, and only afterward found out, he must pay for whatever consecrated thing he desecrated, plus one-fifth.

[17] **if someone should sin** by violating one of the prohibitions, but did not know that what he did was forbidden, he must bring a ram. According to the majority opinion, this is the adjustable guilt-offering; and it applies when someone does not know whether or not he did the forbidden act. The sin-offering applies when he originally did not know that something was forbidden, and found out after his sin. Thus the sin-offering applies as long as he did not know that something was prohibited, until the point when he knew. The guilt-offering applies:

1) when he originally knew that something was forbidden, and then forgot, and afterward remembered again;
2) in the case of the adjustable guilt-offering.

before GOD.

[20]GOD told Moshe: [21]If anyone sins by a breach of faith in GOD: If he dealt falsely with his fellowman regarding a deposit or loan, or he robbed, or oppressed, his fellowman, [22]or if he found a lost article and denied it; and he swore falsely in any case concerning which a man may act, and sins thereby, [23]When he is guilty over sinning, he will return the stolen article that he robbed, or the article concerning which he oppressed, or the deposit that was deposited with him, or the lost article that he found, [24]or whatever he swore falsely about. He will return its principal, and add fifths to it. He will give this to the owner on the day of his guilt, [25]and he will bring to the kohen his guilt-offering to GOD: an unblemished ram from the flock, of the value of a guilt-offering. [26]The kohen will

---

[19] he has incurred guilt before GOD and that explains why it is called a **guilt-offering**

[21] a breach of faith in GOD by doing something wrong to his fellow man **a loan** [literally: an extension of strength] In making someone a partner, one places one's strength at his disposal. **robbed** by force (as in, "he snatched the spear" [II Samuel 23:21]) **oppressed** surreptitiously **his fellowman** [Hebrew: *'amito*] his neighbor, probably so called because they are generally facing [Hebrew: *b'umato*] one another. **[22]** The word **thereby** contains an extra *heh.* **and swore falsely** i.e., *or* swore falsely, regarding money that someone wishes to collect from Him. This interpretation is borne out by the phrase **[24] or whatever he swore falsely about**. The **principal** denotes either the thing itself, or its equivalent in value. **fifths** Use of the plural implies at least two, so two fifths must be added. Later I shall explain this in greater detail [*comment on* Numbers 5:7]. **on the day of his guilt** i.e., he brings the ram on the day that he repents of his guilt. **[25] of value** like the guilt-offering specified earlier [:15]; but he adds *two* fifths because his guilt was intentional (however, there is a single opinion to the effect that this guilt-

secure atonement for him before GOD, and he will be forgiven — for whichever of the above he committed, being guilty thereby.

[6:1]GOD told Moshe: [2]Command Aaron and his sons, saying: "These are the laws of the burnt-offering. It is the burnt-offering that is to be on the pyre on the altar all night till morning. The fire of the altar shall burn upon it. [3]The kohen will put on a smock, and he will put linen pants on his flesh. He will lift up the ashes which the fire consumes of the burnt-offering on the altar, and deposit it beside the Altar. [4]He will remove his garments, put on other garments, and take the ashes outside the camp to a ritually pure place. [5]The fire on the altar will be kept burning: It will not go out. The kohen must burn wood in it each morning. He must arrange the burnt-offering upon it, and he must kindle there the fats of the peace-

---

offering is also adjustable). **[26] being guilty** Scripture makes a noun out of a verb in the *qal* form, instead of using the infinitive.

[6:1] It is the burnt-offering [Hebrew: *'olah*] so called because all of it ascends [Hebrew: *'olah*] up to the Altar. This verse implies that one should not sacrifice the burnt-offering at night, because it must burn on the pyre all night. The word **the pyre** ends in an extra *heh* (or perhaps Hebrew contains both a masculine and a feminine form of the word). **the fire of the altar shall burn upon it** but not outside of it **[3] a smock** [Hebrew: *middo*] The Sages said [Yoma 23b] that this smock was tailored to his measurements [Hebrew: *middato*]. **on his flesh** a euphemism for his genitals (as in, "a flowing from his flesh" [15:2]) **which the fire consumes** i.e., which is left over from what the fire has consumed **beside the Altar** by its eastern side **[5]** This verse repeats **the fire on the altar will be kept burning** in order to add **it must not go out** (during the day). **each morning** [literally: "in the morning, in the morning"] This idiom denotes every morning. First he burns **the burnt-offering**;

offering. [6]A fire must continually be kept burning on the altar: It will not go out.

[7]This is the law of the cereal-offering: The sons of Aaron to offer it before GOD, before the Altar. [8]With his fist he will scoop up some of the fine flour of the cereal-offering, and some of its oil, and all the frankincense on the cereal-offering. He will kindle its memorial-part on the altar as an offering willingly accepted by GOD. [9]Aaron and his sons will eat what is left of it. It must be eaten as maṣṣot in a holy place: They must eat it in the courtyard of the Tent of Assembly. [10]It must not be allowed to leaven. I have given it as their portion of My fire-offerings. It is most holy, as are the sin-offering and the guilt-offering. [11]Every male among the Children of Aaron may eat of it. It is an everlasting portion for all your generations from the fire-offerings of GOD. Whatever touches them will be holy."

[12]GOD told Moshe: [13]This is the offering of Aaron and his descendants, which they will offer to GOD on the day

---

and afterwards **the fats of the peace-offering. [6] A fire must continually be kept** The point of this apparently redundant verse is to add the word **continually**.

[7] This passage supplements what was written in the *parasha* of *Vayyiqra* [2:1]. **to offer** This word is in the infinitive form, and here means *shall offer.* **the sons of Aaron** any one of them, hence Scripture uses the singular **[8] he will scoop up**. **[9] It must be eaten as maṣṣot in a holy place** Thus there are two commandments; and "Every male..." [:11] is a third. **[10] It will not be allowed to leaven** This is the core commandment of Passover. **as are the sin-offering and the guilt-offering** so is the meal-offering. **[11] whatever touches** either the meal-offering, or the sin-offering, or

of his anointment: one-tenth of an *'efa* of fine flour as a perpetual cereal-offering, one half in the morning and the other half in the evening. [14]It must be made well-mixed with oil in a pan. You must bring it baked. You must offer a cereal-offering of well-baked pieces, willingly accepted by GOD. [15]The kohen among his sons who is anointed in his place will perform it. This is an everlasting decree by GOD. It will be burned completely. [16]Every cereal-offering of a kohen will be entirely burned; it will not be eaten.

[17]GOD told Moshe: [18]Tell Aaron and his sons, saying: "This is the law of the sin-offering. The sin-offering must be slaughtered where the burnt-offering is slaughtered be-

---

the guilt-offering, will be holy to GOD.

[13] **This is the offering of Aaron** or one of his descendants after him. **on the day of his anointment** after the anointing oil has been poured on his head. Many people have said that in this phrase the letter *bet* ("on") substitutes for the letter *mem* ("from"): the intent of the verse is that, *from* the day of his anointment, he is obliged to bring his meal-offering continually. [14] **baked** This word has no cognate. Some people say it means "soft", while others say it means "immediately". The *tav* in **you must bring it** and in **you must offer** is the sign of the second person masculine singular future; and in my opinion, so is the *tav* of **well-baked** [Hebrew: *tufiney*], meaning "you will prepare". This word has no cognate. Our ancestors have said [Menaḥot 50b] that it is a compound of two words that mean "you will bake it half-baked" [Hebrew: *tofeh na'*] [the Talmud uses the form *tofehna na'* — Translator]. The grammarian Rabbi Yona ibn Janakh said that the word was similar in form to the word *dukhifat* [11:19], but this is a convoluted etymology. [15] **completely** (i.e., all of it) it belongs completely to GOD [16] **it will not be eaten** as are all other meal-offerings — for how can the kohen eat his own meal-offering or sin-offering?

fore GOD; it is holy, among the holy sacrifices. [19] The kohen who purges it will eat of it. It will be eaten in a holy place: in the courtyard of the Tent of Assembly. [20] Whatever touches its flesh becomes holy. Whatever sprinkles of its blood — you must wash upon the garment which it

---

[18] All sin-offerings are slaughtered toward the North [Zevaḥim 48a–48b]. **holy, among the holy sacrifices** i.e., it is a member of the category of holy sacrifices [*cf. comment on* Genesis 9:25]. [19] **The kohen who purges** denotes the one who dashes the blood — i.e., the one who purges the sinner of his sin. Many commentators have translated this verb in the sense of "to wash", or "to render ritually pure" (as in, "Purge me with hyssop, and I shall be purified" [Psalms 51:9]). [20] **Whatever touches** the flesh of the sin offering will be holy to GOD, and may be eaten by any kohen. Thus, the officiating kohen has an equal share with his fellows. **whatever sprinkles** Rabbi Moshe ben Shmu'el Gikatilla HaKohen said that the verb is in the *qal* form, like "shall bend" [Job 15:29]. When the same verb has a *pataḥ* under the *yod*, it is in the *hif'il* form. In both cases the *nun* of the root disappears. Compare the intransitive "some of her blood sprinkled on the wall" [II Kings 9:33] (with a *ḥiriq*) to the causative "he sprinkled" [8:11] (with a *pataḥ*). Although the verb in "some of her blood sprinkled on the wall" has a *ḥiriq* under the *yod*, it is still in the *qal* form, (which normally takes a *ṣereh* under the *yod* — as in, "their blood sprinkled" [Isaiah 63:3]). Rabbi Moshe HaKohen was correct in asserting all of the above. ¶ Since the peace-offering is holy, GOD commanded us to wash the bloodstain in a holy place — i.e., the Courtyard of the Tent of Assembly (for the word "holy" does not mean the same as the word "ritually pure"). **sprinkle on it**:

- Scripture omits the subject of the first clause ("the spot"), and the connective between the two clauses ("or"). The sentence should read, "*The spot* whereupon any blood should fall on the garment, *or* if any should sprinkle on it...". In other words, if someone else should sprinkle blood on "it" (i.e., the flesh of the sin-offering), the kohen should wash the flesh, and eat it afterward.

or

sprinkles on it, in a holy place. [21]An earthern vessel in which it was cooked must be shattered; but if it was cooked in a copper vessel, it must be scoured and boiled in water. [22]Every male among the kohanim may eat of it; it is most holy. [23]Any sin-offering whose blood is brought into the Tent of Assembly, to secure atonement, into the

---

- Scripture omits the subject of the second clause ("the spot"). The sentence should read, "Should any blood sprinkle on the garment, *the spot* where any falls...". In other words, you must wash the spot where the blood falls. In this case, to function as the feminine object of the preposition in the second clause, the word "garment" must be both feminine and masculine (*cf.* the passage dealing with a former *ṣara'at* sufferer who cannot afford the standard sacrifice, where the word for "turtle-dove" appears both with masculine [14:30] and feminine [14:22] numerical adjectives).

The *tav* in **you must wash** is the sign of the second person masculine singular future. **[21] was cooked** and **scoured** and **boiled** are all verbs in the passive voice. The word **scoured** [Hebrew: *moraq*] has a *ḥolem* over the first consonant of the root (unlike most words in the *pu'al* form), because the second consonant of the root is a *resh.* In Hebrew the *resh,* with very few exceptions, cannot take a strong *dagesh* (compare the similar word "thrown" [Hebrew: *zoraq*] [Numbers 19:13]). **Scoured** is from "polish the spears" [Jeremiah 46:4] — the *mem* is part of the root. **[22]** Only **every male** may eat the sin-offering, because **it is most holy**. Only an unblemished person is fit to eat the sin-offering, which has been brought to secure atonement, and from which a portion has been sacrificed — and the male sex is more perfect than the female sex. Even a minor is called **male** [e.g., Genesis 17:12]; but in the current context, our ancestors have determined that the term denotes someone at least thirteen years old. **[23] Every sacrifice whose blood is brought ... to secure atonement, into the holy place** Here the area outside the Partition is called "holy". Even though the Courtyard is called "holy" [e.g., :9], it is still unholy relative to the Tent of Assembly. The area behind the Partition is also called "holy", since it holy relative to the Tent of Assembly (as in, "With this

holy place, must not be eaten; it must be burnt in fire.

[7:1]This is the law of the guilt-offering: It is most holy. [2]They must slaughter the guilt-offering in the place where they slaughter the burnt-offering, and he must throw its blood all around the sides of the altar. [3]He must offer all the fat from it: the fat-tail, the fat that covers the stomach, [4]the two kidneys, and the fat on them — which is near the loins — and he will remove the lobe on top of the liver, with the kidneys. [5]The kohen will kindle them on the altar, a fire-offering for GOD; it is a guilt-offering. [6]Every male among the kohanim may eat of it. It must be eaten in a holy place; it is most holy. [7]The same law applies to the guilt-offering as to the sin-offering: it belongs to the kohen who purges it. [8]And the kohen who brings a burnt-offering of a man: The skin of the burnt-offering which he brought shall belong to the kohen; it will belong to him. [9]Every oven-baked cereal-offering, and everything prepared in the stewing pan or in the frying pan, shall belong to the kohen who brings it; it

---

shall Aaron enter the holy place:" [16:3]). This sin-offering is the sin-offering of the High Priest [4:3] or of the Sanhedrin [4:14].

[7:1] This is the law of the guilt-offering The reason for mentioning this passage is to discuss suet, which is not mentioned in the laws of the guilt-offering. I have already shown you the difference between "sin" and "guilt" [*comment on* 5:17], even though Scripture sometimes uses the terms interchangeably. **[8] a burnt-offering of** This word is accented on the penultimate syllable, following the rule for nouns in the construct case when the second word is accented on the first syllable. **it shall belong to him** After having stated **it shall belong to the kohen**, Scripture continues its clarification, that the skin may not be given to *another* kohen. **[9] prepared** a feminine adjective, as in "no stone was seen" [I Kings

shall belong to him. [10]Every cereal-offering, mingled with oil or dry, will belong to all the sons of Aaron alike.

[11]This is the law of the peace-offerings one may offer to GOD: [12]If he offers it for thanksgiving, he will offer with the thanksgiving-sacrifice maṣṣa cakes mixed with oil, maṣṣa wafers spread with oil, breads of fine flour drenched with hot oil, [13]and with cakes of leavened bread will he bring his offering — in addition to the sacrifice of his peace-offering for thanksgiving. [14]He will give one of each offering as a donation to GOD; it will belong to the kohen who throws the blood of the peace-offering. [15]The flesh of his peace-offering for thanksgiving will be eaten on the day of his offering; he must leave none of it till morning. [16]If his sacrificial offering is a vow, or a pledge, it must be eaten on the day of his offering his sacrifice; on

---

6:18]. The masculine form of this adjective would be pronounced as in the verse "that which was prepared daily" [Nehemiah 5:18]. **[10] dry** e.g., the adjustable cereal-offering [5:11] and the jealousy-offering [Numbers 5:15].

[12] if he offers it for thanksgiving i.e., he gives thanks to GOD for having escaped a difficulty. **maṣṣa cakes** [*plural*] and also **maṣṣa wafers** [*plural*] as many as he desires, but not fewer than two **fine flour** the interpretations that I prefer render the adjective as "preferred". The **maṣṣa cakes** and the **maṣṣa wafers** are baked; the **breads of fine flour** are not. **[13] with cakes** [literally: on cakes] as in "the men came with the women" [literally: on the women] [Exodus 35:22]. **[14] he will give one of each** Thus there are at least four cakes (but actually there are at least ten [Menaḥot 77b]). **[15] will be eaten on the day of his offering** Among the person who brought it, and his family, only those who are ritually pure may eat it: for even the peace-offering is holy, albeit a lower degree of holiness. **[16] a vow** which is uttered in distress **a pledge** a spirit of largess prompted him to bring an offering to GOD. This

the day following, what remains may be eaten. [17]What remains then of the flesh of the sacrifice must be burnt on the third day. [18]If the flesh of the peace-offering is eaten on the third day, it will not be accepted; it will not be accounted to the owner; it will be offensive; the person who eats of it will carry his iniquity. [19]Meat that touches any ritually impure thing must not be eaten; it must be burned in fire. Anyone who is ritually pure may eat of the meat. [20]A person who eats of the meat of a peace-offering to GOD while he is ritually impure — that person

---

is neither the fulfillment of a vow, nor an offering of gratitude. **of his offering** The verb is an infinitive of the *hif'il* form. **the day following** i.e., the day following the day of his offering. The *vav* in **what remains** is a general-purpose connective particle, like the *f* of Arabic. **[17] will be burnt** but not on the Altar, where the parts of the animal sacrifices were burnt [3:5] **[18] it will not be accounted to the owner** After parts of it are offered to the Most High, everything that remains becomes holy (likewise, after stones for the Altar become holy, it is improper for there to be anything unholy left over — that is why unhewn stones must be used [Exodus 20:22][1]). **offensive** as in, "broth of abominable things is in their vessels" [Isaiah 65:4]. Onkelos translated this word correctly into the Aramaic "meraḥaq". Some people have wondered how the sacrifice can be of no account once it has been "willingly accepted" [3:5]. Clearly, it is the intention of the sacrificer that determines the acceptance of the sacrifice. Someone who expected to eat from the peace-offering on the third day never intended to bring a valid peace-offering; for the peace-offerings are intrinsically holy, while the **offensive** leftovers are intrinsically unholy. Moreover, whatever gain he receives from fulfilling the commandment is offset by the loss he suffers from *not* fulfilling the commandment, in the case of a peace-offering. In the case of a vow, since he did not fulfill his obligation, his original delinquency is reactivated. **he will carry his iniquity** i.e., he will suffer the unspecified punishment. **[20]** The punishment for eating *any* holy food while ritually impure is *karet*

[1] [See also Deuteronomy 27:6]

will be cut off from his people. [21]A person who touches any ritual impurity (whether a ritual impurity of man, or a ritually impure beast, or any ritually impure creeping creature) and then eats of the flesh of a peace-offering to GOD — that person will be cut off from his people." [22]GOD told Moshe: [23]Tell the Children of Israel: Never

---

[22:3] [Karetot 2b]. **while he is ritually impure** either an *intrinsic* ritual impurity (e.g., someone who suffers from a constant flow, someone who has *ṣara'at*, or even a man who has had a nocturnal emission[1]) or a *derived* ritual impurity (e.g., ritual impurity acquired from a corpse, or from someone who suffers from a constant flow, or from someone who has *ṣara'at*, or from a quadruped that is unfit for food, or from a ritually impure flying or crawling animal). **[23]** Once a certain Sadducee [a derogatory reference to a Karaite — Translator] approached me and asked if the Torah forbade eating the fat-tail. I told him the truth, saying that although the fat-tail falls within the category of suet (as it is written: "its suet: the entire fat-tail..." [3:9]), our ancestors permitted it to be eaten and forbade all other suet. He then replied, Doesn't the Torah prohibit *all* suet? — for it is written: "Eat no suet or blood" [3:17]; and this injunction is preceded by, "it is an everlasting decree for your generations..." [3:17]. I answered that the abovementioned verse appears in the context of the peace-offering. The phrase, "it is an everlasting decree for your generations in all your dwelling places" is not an irrefutable proof of his thesis, since Scripture also says, "You will eat [from the new crop] neither bread, nor parched grain, nor kernels, until that very day, until you bring the offering of your God" [23:14] — and there Scripture *also* says, "it is an everlasting decree...". By this reasoning, we may not eat bread in Exile, since we have not brought the 'Omer offering! He continued to argue, citing, **Never eat the suet of cattle, sheep, and goats**. I continued to refute him, pointing out that this verse also appears in the context of the peace-offering. My evidence is the qualifier in "Whoever eats the suet of animals that are brought as offerings to GOD" [:25]. Consider the consequences of his reasoning: the

---

[1] As it is written: "he thought, 'it is an accidental pollution...'" [I Samuel 20:26]

eat the suet of cattle, sheep, and goats. [24]The suet of an animal that dies by itself and the suet of an animal that has been torn may be used for any purpose other than eating. [25]Whoever eats the suet from a beast of which one may offer a fire-offering to GOD — the person who eats will be cut off from his people. [26]Nor will you eat blood of either fowl or beasts in any of your settlements. [27]Whoever eats any blood will be cut off from his people.

[28]GOD told Moshe: [29]Tell the Children of Israel: "Whoever offers his peace-offerings to GOD will himself bring to GOD his peace-offering. [30]His own hands will bring GOD's fire-offering: He will bring the suet upon the breast

---

abovementioned qualifier is now needed only to exclude from the prohibition all meat that is not brought as a peace-offering (i.e., ordinary meat). Accordingly, this *parasha* specifies that **[24] the suet of an animal that dies by itself** [Hebrew: *neveylah*] **and the suet of an animal that has been torn** [Hebrew: *ṭereyfah*] **may be used for any purpose other than eating.** The meat of a *neveylah* and of a *ṭereyfah* are elsewhere known to be forbidden [Deuteronomy 14:21; Exodus 22:30]; but it is the *meat* that is prohibited. Since the suet of such an animal is not brought on top of the Altar, one might think that it is permissible for food — hence the verse admonishes, **other than eating**. Consequently, Scripture did not need to repeat the prohibition against blood; and this passage was written to teach us the punishment for eating the suet of sanctified animals. Likewise, the verse **[26] Nor will you eat blood...** exists only to incorporate birds in the prohibition — this is why the suet of birds is permissible [Karetot 4a]. The conclusive proof is that the Book of Deuteronomy mentions that meat of luxury (i.e., ordinary meat) is completely permissible, and in three different places excludes only the blood [Deuteronomy 12:23; 12:24; 12:25] — without *any* mention of suet! At this point the eyes of the Sadducee [a derogatory reference to a Karaite — Translator] were opened, and an oath escaped his lips, that he would not rely on his own reasoning for the derivation of the Commandments, but that he would depend on the

with the breast, to wave it as a wave-offering before GOD. [31]The kohen will kindle the suet on the altar, but the breast will be Aaron's and his sons'. [32]You must give the right thigh as a donation to the kohen from your peace-offerings. [33]Whoever offers the blood of the peace-offering and the suet, among the sons of Aaron — to him the right thigh shall be apportioned. [34]For I have taken the breast that is waved and the thigh that is donated from the peace-offerings of the Children of Israel, and I have given them to Aaron the kohen and to his sons as a permanent portion from the Children of Israel. [35]This is the reward of Aaron and the reward of his sons from GOD's fire-offerings, on the day they were presented to officiate before GOD, [36]which GOD commanded to give them, on the day of their anointment, from the children of Israel; it is an everlasting decree for all their generations." [37]These are the laws of the burnt-offering, of the cereal-offering, of the sin-offering, of the guilt-offering; of the installation- and of the peace-offering, [38]which GOD commanded Moshe at Mount Sinai, on the day He commanded the Children of Israel to present their offerings to GOD in the

---

exegesis of the traditional commentators.

[33] The right thigh goes to the one who sprinkles the blood; while the breast [:31] goes to all of the kohanim. **[35] This** I.e., this is the reward for Aaron's consecration, and his sons' consecration — patrimony. **[37] installation** as it is written in the *parasha* of *Teṣavveh* [Exodus 29] **[38] to present their offerings to GOD in the Sinai Desert** for they did not offer a sacrifice before they arrived at Mount Sinai. I have already shown you [*comment on* Exodus 17:15] that the altar that Moshe built on the occasion of 'Amaleq's defeat was situated at Ḥorev (i.e., Sinai). Israel remained there for ten days under a year, as it is written [Exodus 19:1 *vs.* Numbers 10:11]. Moreover, they did not bring burnt-offerings

Sinai Desert.

[8:1]GOD told Moshe: [2]"Invite Aaron with his sons; and take the garments, the oil for anointing, the bullock sin-offering, the two rams, and the basket of the maṣṣot; [3]and gather all of the community at the entrance of the Tent of Assembly." [4]Moshe did as GOD commanded him, and the community gathered at the entrance of the Tent of Assembly. [5]Moshe told the community: "This is what GOD commanded to do." [6]Moshe led Aaron and his sons, and he washed them with water. [7]He put the tunic on him, and girded him with the belt. He dressed him in the robe, and put the ephod on him, and he tied the ephod around him with its belt. [8]He placed the breast-plate on him. He placed the 'Urim and Tummim on the breast-plate. [9]He set the turban on his head, and over the tur-

---

while they were in the wilderness (as the prophet said, "Did you bring me sacrifices and offerings for forty years in the wilderness?" [Amos 5:25]). The families of Israel also did not bring the Paschal sacrifice (except in Egypt, and a second time at Mount Sinai) because they had no flocks in the wilderness. Nor did they perform any circumcisions once they had left Mount Sinai; and the majority were uncircumcised when Joshua had them circumcised for the sake of the Paschal sacrifice [Joshua 5:3].

[8:2] the bullock sin-offering Scripture uses the definite article because it has already been mentioned [Exodus 29:1]. Likewise, **the rams** and **the maṣṣot**. **[3] all of the community** denotes the heads of the tribes and the elders. **[6] Moshe led Aaron** to the laver. **he washed them** i.e., he commanded them to wash **[7] and he secured the ephod** this verb is redundant in meaning with **he tied the ephod**. **[8]** Just as the golden ṣiṣ is different from the turban, the 'Urim and Tummim are not the stones of the breastplate. The Tablets are similarly not a part of the ark into which they were placed. Scripture accordingly says that the 'Urim and Tummim

ban, in front, he placed the golden ṣiṣ, the holy crown, as GOD had ordered Moshe.
[10]Moshe took the anointment oil, and anointed the Divine Tent and all that was in it, and he consecrated them.
[11]He sprinkled some of it on the altar seven times; he anointed the altar and all its vessels, and the laver and its stand, to consecrate them.
[12]He poured some anointment oil on Aaron's head, and anointed him, to consecrate him.
[13]Moshe led the sons of Aaron. He dressed them in tunics, girded them with linen belts, and tied hoods on them, as GOD had commanded Moshe.
[14]He brought the bullock sin-offering, and Aaron and his sons placed their hands on the bullock's head.
[15]He slaughtered it. Moshe took the blood, and put it all around the corners of the altar with his finger, purifying the altar; he poured out the blood at the base of the altar, sanctifying it to thereby secure atonement.
[16]He took all the fat on the stomach, the lobe of the liver, and the two kidneys with their suet, and Moshe kindled it on the altar.
[17]But the bullock — its skin, its flesh, and its dung — he burned in a fire outside the camp, as GOD had commanded

---

were placed *on* the breastplate. **[10] Moshe took the anointment oil** meaning, Moshe *had taken* the oil, prior to Aaron's anointment. **[13] Moshe led the sons of Aaron** Scripture appears to belabor the point. Perhaps Moshe led them a second time; or, perhaps the verse means, "*When* Moshe led the sons of Aaron..." **he dressed them** a transitive verb with both a direct and an indirect object **[15] purifying** explained above [*comment on* Exodus 29:14] **sanctifying** for the atonement of all sins **[16] He took all the fat on the stomach** the earlier verse [7:3] has "that *covers* the stomach"; yet another verse [3:3] says, "that covers the stomach, and all the fat on the stomach." Understand the following: a great deal of fat covers the stomach, while only a small amount of fat, here and there, is actually *on* the stomach. Moreover, fat that *covers* the stomach can also be said to be *on* the stomach. For these reasons,

Moshe. [18]He brought the ram for the burnt-offering, and Aaron and his sons placed their hands on the ram's head. [19]He slaughtered it. Moshe threw the blood around the sides of the altar. [20]He cut the ram into pieces, and Moshe kindled the head, the pieces, and the fats. [21]He washed the stomach and the two legs with water. Moshe kindled all of the ram on the altar, a burnt-offering willingly accepted and consumed by fire for GOD, as GOD had commanded Moshe. [22] He brought the other ram, the ram of installation, and Aaron and his sons placed their hands on the ram's head. [23] He slaughtered it. Moshe took some of its blood, and put it upon the lobe of Aaron's right ear, and upon the thumb of his right hand, and upon the big toe of his right foot. [24] He brought Aaron's sons. Moshe put some of the blood upon the lobes of their right ears,

---

Scripture employs brevity here. **[17] he burned in a fire** some say he burned it himself; others say he commanded others to burn it. Those of the former opinion bring the words, **as GOD had commanded Moshe** as evidence. This evidence is inconclusive, since Hebrew often attributes action to indirect agents. **[22] He brought the other ram, the ram of installation, and Aaron and his sons placed** [*plural*] **their hands** the earlier verse [Exodus 29:19] has, "Aaron and his sons shall place [*singular*] their hands....". No difference in meaning here exists between the singular and plural forms of the verb. A great grammarian erred when he said that the meaning of the singular was that he alone was to place his hands first, followed by his sons; and that the plural meant that they all placed their hands together. **[23] right** this feminine adjective modifies the first of two nouns, as in "the inner [*feminine*] gate [*feminine*] of the court [*masculine*]" [I Kings 7:12]. I shall give the reason for the **lobe** and the **thumb** in the *parasha* of *Meṣora'* [*comment on* 14:14]. We see here that blood secures atonement for Aaron's soul, as it is stated: "for the blood atones with the soul" [17:11] – meaning, it atones through the spirit of life which it formerly contained, in the sense of "a soul for a soul" [Exodus 21:23]. The phrase "she cast it down at his feet" [Exodus 4:25] ad-

upon the thumbs of their right hands, and upon the big toes of their right feet, and Moshe threw the blood around the sides of the altar. [25]He took the suet, the fat-tail, all the fat on the stomach, the lobe of the liver, the two kidneys and their fat, and the right thigh. [26]From the basket of maṣṣot before GOD, he drew one maṣṣa cake, one cake of oiled bread, and one wafer. He placed them on the fats, and upon the right thigh. [27]He arranged all this on Aaron's hands and on his sons' hands, and he waved them as a wave-offering before GOD. [28]Moshe took them from their hands, and kindled them on the altar in addition to the burnt-offering; they were an installation, willingly accepted; it was consumed by fire for GOD. [29]Moshe took the breast, and waved it as a wave-offering before GOD. It was Moshe' portion of the ram of installation; as GOD had commanded Moshe. [30]Moshe took some anointment oil and some of the blood from the altar, and sprinkled on Aaron and on his garments, and on his sons and on their garments with him, and he consecrated Aaron, his garments, his sons, and his sons' garments with him. [31]Moshe told Aaron and his sons: "Cook the flesh at the entrance to the Tent of Assembly, and eat it there with the bread that is in the basket of installation, as I was or-

---

dresses a similar idea. **[26] one maṣṣa cake** this is the "one loaf of bread" [Exodus 29:23]. "Loaf" [Hebrew: *kikkar*] is probably a unit of weight, but not the *kikkar* used to weigh gold and silver. **he placed them on the fats** Scripture does not mention the lobe and the kidneys, because the lobe is small (it literally means "surplus") and the kidneys were together with their fats. It is unlikely that the term "fats" ever literally denotes the kidneys, although it can denote the tail. **[27] he waved them** he waved Aaron and his sons, just as Aaron was to wave the Levites [Numbers 8:11]. **[31] Cook the flesh** they personally ("You shall...cook its flesh" [Exodus

dered: 'Aaron and his sons will eat it.' [32] What remains of the meat and the bread, you will burn in fire. [33] You will not leave the entrance to the Tent of Assembly for seven days, until the completion day of your days of installation, because seven days you shall be installed. [34] GOD has commanded to do that which was done this

---

29:31] means that Moshe is to give the command.) **[32] What remains of the meat and the bread** by next morning, as written [Exodus 29:34] **[33] you shall be installed** the clause omits "at the end of". Scripture means to say that at the end of seven days, they shall be installed. ¶Some people say that they did not leave for seven *days*, but that during the night they used to leave to tend to their personal necessities. My personal belief is that they could leave when they needed to, day or night. A great scholar said that they dug a latrine in the courtyard of the Tent of Assembly, but this is far-fetched. Scripture says, "The children of Israel wept for Moshe...thirty days." [Deuteronomy 34:8] — was there never a moment when they were not crying? By saying that they should stay in the entrance to the Tent of Assembly day and night [:35] Scripture means only to say that they should not concern themselves with other business, and that they should not take walks to any other places. (Compare to, "he will not leave the Sanctuary" [21:12] as I will explain later.) **[34] That which was done this day** GOD commanded Moshe to do what he had done this day throughout the seven days of installation. Moshe should have said, "that which I have done"; but Hebrew often abruptly changes from the first person to the third person (as in, "Ezekiel shall be a sign for you" [Ezekiel 24:24]; "...and Yiftaḥ, and Samuel" [I Samuel 12:11]). **GOD has commanded** Where was this made explicit? In the passage "Thus shall you do for Aaron and his sons, according to all that I have commanded you, for seven days..." [Exodus 29:35], and furthermore, "You shall offer a bullock as a sin-offering by day" [Exodus 29:36] (the phrase "by day" here means "day by day", as in "two daily: this is the perpetual burnt-offering" [Numbers 28:3]). Scripture continues with the words "you shall sprinkle the blood of the sin-offering ... and anoint it" [Exodus 29:26] — this is to be done daily, until the end of the consecration period — and finally "Seven days you shall perform atonement on

day to make atonement for you. [35] Within the Tent of Assembly you will stay day and night for seven days, and keep the watch of GOD, so that you will not die; for so was I commanded." [36] Aaron and his sons did everything GOD had commanded through Moshe.

[9:1] On the eighth day Moshe called Aaron, and his sons, and the elders of Israel. [2] He said to Aaron: "Bring for yourself a young calf as a sin-offering and a ram as a burnt-offering, without a defect, and offer them before

---

the altar" [Exodus 29:27]. Notice that this passage employs brevity, and does not explicitly mention the two rams. Many people consequently arrived at the opinion that only the bullock sacrifice was repeated throughout the seven-day period. However, I believe that Scripture singles out the bullock sacrifice because the upcoming passage deals with the sanctification of the altar. The ram burnt-offering provided blood which was sprinkled on Aaron and on his sons, while the second ram provided meat to be eaten; but only the bullock sin-offering secured atonement for the altar. For this reason, the bullock offering is described "with atonement" [Exodus 29:36] – i.e., for the sake of atonement. **[35] Within the Tent of Assembly you will stay** repeated in order to mention the death penalty. **I was commanded** a verb in the passive voice. Some people say that this refers to "according to all that I have commanded you," [Exodus 29:35] even though there Scripture does not explain that Aaron and his sons were to stay in the entrance to the Tent of Assembly.

[9:1] On the eighth day We might suppose that by "the eighth day" the eighth day of Nisan is meant, since the Tabernacle was erected on the first day of the month. However, the Exegetes said that this occurred on the first day of Nisan, and that during each of the seven days of installation Moshe had erected the Tabernacle and destroyed it, in order to accustom the people to it and to instruct them [*see Torat Kohanim* on this verse]. **Moshe called Aaron and his sons** who then left the entrance of the Tent of Assembly, or perhaps the leaders came into the courtyard. **[2] a**

**GOD. [3]You will tell the Children of Israel as follows:
'Bring a he-goat as a sin-offering, a calf and a lamb,
within their first year, unblemished, as a burnt-offering;
[4]and an ox and a ram as peace-offerings, to sacrifice before GOD; also a cereal-offering mixed with oil — for today GOD will be revealed to you.'" [5]They brought what
Moshe had ordered to the front of the Tent of Assembly.
The whole community approached, and stood before GOD.
[6]Moshe had said: "This is the thing that GOD has commanded you to do; the Glory of GOD will be revealed to
you." [7]Moshe said to Aaron: "Approach the altar, offer
your sin-offering and your burnt-offering, and secure
atonement for youself and for the people. Then present
the offering of the people and atone for them, as GOD
commanded." [8]Aaron approached the altar, and**

---

young calf During the seven days of installation they brought a young *bullock* as a sin-offering [Exodus 29:1] and a ram as a burnt-offering [Exodus 29:18]. Scripture does not specify here whether use of the term *calf* denotes an animal under one year of age. I believe, though, that "bullock" and "calf" are probably similar in meaning when an age is not mentioned. **without a defect** describes both the calf and the ram. ¶The bullocks of installation atoned for the Altar, while this calf is to atone for Aaron (I have already explained the meaning of the word "atone"). **[4] an ox and a ram** full-grown. **cereal-offering** the appropriate amount of fine flour for each one of the sacrifices. **[6] Moshe had said** I have already explained regarding "I asked her" [Genesis 24:47] that the verb is in the past perfect tense, as it is here. Moshe had already told them what GOD commanded — that they must offer a goat, and a bullock, and a lamb, and an ox, and a ram — prior to the appearance of the Glory of GOD (i.e., the fire on the altar). **[7] secure atonement for yourself and for the people** i.e., you are required to atone for yourself and for the congregation. You will secure atonement for yourself by the sin-offering of a bull; afterwards, you will bring the nation's offering and secure atonement for them. No man can

slaughtered the calf of sin-offering which was his. [9]The sons of Aaron brought the blood to him, and he dipped his finger in the blood, and placed it on the corners of the altar. He poured the blood at the base of the altar. [10]The fat, the kidneys, and the lobe from the liver of the sin-offering, he kindled on the altar, as GOD had commanded Moshe. [11]The flesh and the skin he burned in fire outside the camp. [12]He slaughtered the burnt-offering. Aaron's sons handed him the blood, and he threw it around the altar. [13]They handed him the burnt-offering in limbs, then its head. He kindled it on the altar. [14]He washed the innards and the legs, and he kindled them with the burnt-offering on the altar. [15]He offered the people's offering. He took the goat that was the people's sin-offering, slaughtered it, and made atonement with it as with the previous sin-offering. [16]He brought the burnt-offering, and treated it according to form. [17]He brought the cereal-offering, filled his hand from it, and kindled it on the altar, in addition to the morning burnt-offering. [18]He slaughtered the ox and the ram, the people's peace-offering. The sons of Aaron handed him the blood, and he threw it around the altar; [19]and the fats of the ox; and from the ram the fat-tail, that which covers, the kidneys,

---

atone for another until he is cleansed of all sin himself. **[8] his** It was from his own property, as is the bull of Yom Kippur [16:6]. **[9] he poured the blood** that remained **[10] the fat** all three fats:

1) the fat that covers the stomach;
2) the fat that is on the stomach;
3) the fat that is on the kidneys

[13] handed him In Hebrew the literal meaning of the verb is "caused him to find". This form is used because a bullock which met the age and appearance specifications had to be *found.* **[15] he offered the people's offering** he brought it to the altar **made atonement** obtained forgiveness for sins **the previous sin-offering** the

and the lobe of the liver. [20]They put the fats on the breasts, and he kindled the fats on the altar. [21]Aaron waved the breasts and the right thigh as a wave-offering before GOD, as Moshe had commanded. [22]Aaron spread out his hands toward the people, and blessed them; and he stepped off after he had finished sacrificing the sin-offering, the burnt-offering, and the peace-offering. [23]Moshe and Aaron entered the Tent of Assembly. When they came out they blessed the people. The Glory of GOD revealed Itself to all the people, [24]and fire descended from before GOD, and consumed upon the altar the burnt-offering and the fats. When the people beheld it, they offered praise, and fell upon their faces. [10:1]The sons of Aaron Nadav and 'Avihu each took his coal-pan, put fire in it, and placed incense on it; and they offered unconsecrated fire before GOD, which He had not commanded

---

bullock **[20] They put the fats** with the kidneys and the lobe of the liver, as I have explained [*comment on* 8:26]. **[21] the breasts** the breast of the ox and the breast of the ram **the right thigh** since "thigh" is a feminine noun and "right" is in masculine form, the former must be in the construct case with an implied possessor, i.e., "the thigh [of the] right [side]". **[22] spread out his hands toward the people** Our ancestors used this verse [Soṭa 38a] to derive exegetically the appearance of the hands during the Priestly Blessing. **he stepped off** As I have pointed out in many similar places, this verb is in the past perfect tense. Aaron had already stepped off the altar, having done the people's sin-offering, and their burnt-offering, and their peace-offering. ¶Scripture says that **he stepped off** because the Altar was three cubits high. Moshe and Aaron went from there into the Tent of Assembly — probably to pray for the appearance of the fire — and when they came out, they both blessed the people. **[24] the burnt-offering** Aaron's burnt-offering, as well as the people's burnt-offering and the daily burnt-offering (We know the last had also been given because of continual reappearance of the words "besides the burnt-offering of each morn-

them. [2]Fire descended from before GOD and consumed them; they died before GOD. [3]Moshe said to Aaron: "This is what GOD told me to say: 'I will be sanctified by those who are near to Me. In the presence of all the nation, I shall be glorified.'" Aaron was silent. [4]Moshe called Misha'el and 'Elṣafan, sons of Uziel the uncle of Aaron, and said to them: "Come near, carry your kinfolk out of the holy place, out of the camp." [5]They came near, and pulled them by their tunics to beyond the camp, as Moshe had instructed. [6]Moshe told Aaron and his sons, 'El'azar and 'Itamar: "Do not crinify your heads, and do not cleave your garments, so that you will not die, and He rage against the whole community. Your brethren the whole house of Israel will bewail the burning that GOD

---

ing" [e.g., Numbers 28:23]). **[10:1] his coal-pan** each one took his own coal-pan. In my opinion, this event also occurred "on the eighth day"; and this is borne out later on: "...they had already sacrificed their sin-offering...today" [:19]. **put fire in it** this fire was not taken from the fire that had descended from GOD [9:24] — it was "unconsecrated fire". **which He had not commanded them** both the burning of the incense *and* the use of unconsecrated fire were their own idea, not a commandment. **[2] they died before GOD** thinking they were doing something acceptable to GOD **[3] This is what GOD has told me** GOD has already told me that he will manifest his holiness through those who are near Him — even if they must suffer for it, as in the passage "You only have I known..." [Amos 3:2]. Thus the verse means, "When I manifest myself in holiness among them, then I shall be glorified; and I shall be glorified in the face of all the people, and they shall fear Me." **[4] carry your kinfolk out of the holy place** Some say that the incense had been brought to the sacrificial altar, where the Levites could go; others say that it had been brought to the incense-altar, and that Moshe brought the bodies out of the Tent of Assembly. **holy place** this was the Courtyard, in view of the camp, as I have explained [9:1]. **[6] Do not crinify your heads** Some say that this denotes growing long hair. **do not cleave your garments** i.e., do

has kindled. [7]You shall not leave the entrance of the Tent of Assembly, so that you will not die, for the anointment-oil of GOD is upon you." They did according to Moshe's words.

[8]GOD told Aaron: [9]"You must not drink wine or strong drink, neither you nor your sons with you, when you enter the Tent of Assembly, so that you not die; this is an everlasting decree throughout your generations. [10]To distinguish between holy and unholy, and between ritually im-

---

not tear your garments. This word is also found in the passage "he will wear torn clothes and his hair will grow wild" [13:45]. (Some say the former adjective means "covered"; others say it means "uncovered"; but the traditional meaning is correct.) **so that you will not die** "Not" takes a compound object here (compare "I have not learned knowledge, and understood holiness" [Proverbs 30:3]) as if Scripture had said "...and He *not* rage against the whole community". The reason for such consequences is that the kohanim were needed to atone for the entire community. **your brethren the whole house of Israel** The inclusion of Levites in the house of Israel is alluded to in the *parasha* of *R'eh* [Deuteronomy 12:17].

[8] GOD told Aaron Aaron, too, was a prophet (though some say that GOD spoke to him indirectly through Moshe, just as Scripture says elsewhere that GOD spoke to Aḥaz [Isaiah 6:10]). GOD warns him to be careful not to die like his two eldest sons. **[9] or strong drink** which is made from certain kinds of grain, or honey, or dates. Wine destroys the understanding of him who drinks it, and he becomes mixed-up. You are the High Priest, and you must be able **[10] to distinguish** between holy places and unholy places ("unholy" [Hebrew: *ḥol*] comes from the word "profane" [Hebrew: *ḥillul*]), as well as between holy days and unholy days. **ritually impure and ritually pure** including beasts and water-creatures and birds. Accordingly, the section beginning with "these are the animals..." [11:2] immediately follows; and it in turn is followed by various other types of ritual impurity:

a new mother [12:2];

pure and ritually pure. [11]and to teach the Children of Israel all the decrees that GOD has told them through Moshe."

[12]Moshe told Aaron and his remaining sons 'El'azar and 'Itamar: "Take the cereal-offering that remains of the offerings to be consumed by fire for GOD, and eat it as maṣṣot, beside the altar, for it is most holy. [13]You will eat it in a holy place, because it is your share and the share of your sons from GOD's fire-offerings; for so I was commanded. [14]The waved breast and the donated thigh you will eat in a ritually pure place — you and your sons and your daughters with you, for they are given as your share and your sons' share of the peace-offerings of the

---

ṣara'at of man [13:2] or clothes [13:47] or houses [14:34];
a man who has had a seminal emission [15:16];
a man [15:2] or woman [15:25] who has a continual discharge; and
a menstruant [15:19]
— all this is meant here by "distinguish between ritually pure and ritually impure".

[11] teach the children of Israel all the other commandments (compare, "everything that the kohanim will teach you" [Deuteronomy 24:8])

[12] Take the cereal-offering Once incense has been taken from it and offered to the Most High, the remainder must be eaten in holiness [*comment on* 7:18]. **[13]** From now on, you are to eat the portion which GOD has forever given you **from GOD's fire-offerings. [14] a ritually pure place** It may even be outside of the Courtyard. Both the males and the females among you may eat the breast and the thigh (as it is written: "Everyone in your house who is ritually pure may eat of it" [Numbers 18:11]), as well as slaves whom you have purchased, slaves who have been born in your house, and widows who have returned to your household. The breast and the thigh, which you are eating now, will be your portion

Children of Israel. [15]They will bring the donated thigh and the waved breast upon the fire-offering fats, to wave them as a wave-offering before GOD; and it will be yours and your sons' with you, an everlasting portion, as GOD commanded." [16]Moshe inquired about the goat sin-offering: It had been burned. He was angry with 'El'azar and 'Itamar, the remaining sons of Aaron, saying: [17]"Why have you not eaten the sin-offering in the holy place, as it is most holy, and He has given it to you to pardon the iniquity of the assembly, to atone for them before GOD? [18]Its blood was not brought into the inner court of the Sanctuary. You should certainly have eaten it in the holy place as I commanded." [19]Aaron spoke to Moshe: "They had already sacrificed their sin-offering and their burnt-offering today before GOD. When these befell me — if I were to eat the sin-offering today, would it have

---

from all peace-offerings. **[16] burned** a verb in the passive voice. Its form is similar to "scoured" and "boiled" [6:21]. **[17] in the holy place** at the entrance to the Tent of Assembly, as it is written [9:31]. **and He** (GOD) **has given it to you to pardon** [literally: **carry away**]:

- When you eat the sin-offering, *GOD* will carry away the sin of the congregation; or
- *You* shall carry off the sin (meaning, their sins shall be forgiven through you — this explains the concluding clause, "to atone...")

[18] Its blood was not brought into the inner court of the Sanctuary unlike the bull that atones for all of the commandments, and which can be brought by the High Priest [4:4] or by the entire congregation [4:14]. One might point out that there *is* one sin-offering of a bull that is entirely burned, but whose blood is *not* brought into the inner court (i.e., the golden altar, in front of the Partition) [Exodus 29:14]. Understand, though, that that bull was a sin-offering for the Altar. This goat, on the other hand, was a sin-offering for the people; therefore, its meat belongs to the kohen.

pleased GOD?" [20]When Moshe heard, he was pleased.

You should certainly have eaten it it was proper for you to eat it [19] Many grammarians have said that the interrogatory *heh* doubles the consonant that follows it only when the consonant is pronounced with a voiced schwa, but not with any of the seven other vowels. In such a case the *heh* is pronounced with a *pataḥ* because the language will not permit two voiced semi-vowels to follow one another. Because the *yod* in **would it have pleased** [Hebrew: *hayyiṭav*] is doubled, they say that the *heh* must be the sign of the definite article, as in "the one that came back with Naomi" [Ruth 2:6], "the ones that are present here" [I Chronicles 29:17], and "the city that was strong" [Ezekiel 26:17]. There the *heh* acts as a relative pronoun, and they say the same is true here with *hayyiṭav*. They also say that the verb **if I were to eat** is really in the simple past tense — if it were in the subjunctive, it would be stressed on the final syllable (compare, "I *have spoken* by the prophets" [Hosea 12:11] and "I *shall speak* to you" [Exodus 25:22]) — and that Aaron refers to *their* (his burnt sons') sin-offering and *their* burnt-offering because the calf and the ram were for Aaron and his sons. **When these befell me** the implied subject is the concern or the anguish over the death of the sons. Because of this, I was unable to eat all of the sin-offering. I only ate "that which was pleasing [Hebrew: *hayyiṭav*] to GOD" — meaning, the minimum that would relieve me of my obligation. ¶Those Exegetes who maintain that the *heh* in *hayyiṭav* is interrogatory perforce imply that the word is irregular. The same is also true of the explanation which I mentioned above, since in all of Scripture we do not find the *heh* of the definite article used as a relative pronoun in conjunction with a verb in the future tense. If the former Exegetes are correct, then we must translate **if I were to eat** — using the future tense as the subjunctive. We *do* find such words in the future tense accented on the penultimate syllable (e.g., "lest I be poor, and steal" [Proverbs 30:9]). In such a case, Aaron's meaning would be: I was a mourner who had not yet buried his dead; and a mourner who has not yet buried his dead may not eat from the sin-offering (compare to, "I have not eaten of it in my mourning" [Deuteronomy 26:14]).

[11:1] GOD told Moshe and Aaron because Aaron was the ko-

**[11:1]GOD told Moshe and Aaron, saying to them: [2]Tell
the Children of Israel: "You may eat these animals from
among all beasts that are on land: [3]Anything hoofed
with hooves, and the hooves are split, and is cud-chewing,
among the beasts — you may eat it. [4]But do not eat the
following, among the ruminants, and among the hoofed
animals: the camel — although it ruminates, its hoofs are
not split — is ritually impure for you; [5]the cony —
although it ruminates, its hoofs are not split — is ritually
impure for you; [6]the hare — although it ruminates, its
hoofs are not split — is ritually impure for you; [7]and the
swine, although it is hoofed, and its hoofs are completely
split — it does not ruminate; it is ritually impure for you.
[8]Do not eat of their flesh, and do not touch their remains; they are ritually impure for you. [9]Of all that is
in the water, you may eat these: anything that has fins
and scales in the water, in the seas and in the streams —**

---

hen, who must teach others how to distinguish between ritually impure and ritually pure **[3] hoofed** an adjective, as in "horned and hoofed" [Psalms 69:32], denoting anything that can be said to have a hoof. **split** an adjective, denoting an animal whose hoofs are split. **cud-chewing** "cud" [Hebrew: *gera*] is derived from the word "throat" [Hebrew: *garon*]. **chewing** a verb **[4]** Scripture mentions the camel, the cony, the hare, and the swine, because each of these species displays exactly one of the signs. **[6]** The Hebrew language generally uses the name of the male of the species as a generic term which includes the female as well. Here Scripture uses the term for a female cony — some say because the male is rarely seen, some say because the male becomes female and back again. The former explanation seems more probable. **[8] do not touch their remains** Scripture does not mention that someone who *does* touch their remains is ritually impure until evening, but we know this from tradition. Moreover, it is a corporal offense to touch their remains deliberately, since by so doing, one violates a prohibition [see also Deuteronomy 14:8]. **[9]** If we were to follow the literal

them you may eat. [10]Anything that does not have fins and scales, in the seas and in the streams, among all that swarm in the water, and among all that live in the water, are a detestation to you. [11]They will be a detestation to you: You may not eat their flesh. You will detest their remains. [12]Whatever has no fins or scales in the water is a detestation to you. [13]Of the fowl you will detest these — they will not be eaten; they are a detestation: the *nesher*,

---

meaning of the verse, without exegetical explanation, we would not permit ourselves to eat fish that are found in lakes, since the verse specifies seas and streams only. **fins and scales** following the traditional Aramaic rendition of the words **[10] that swarm in the water** tiny creatures that originate in the water **that live in the water** creatures that originate from a male and a female **[11]** After having said "they are a detestation to you" [:10] Scripture says, **they will be a detestation to you** to specify what the word "detestation" signifies — i.e., that **you may not eat their flesh.**[1] **[12]** The apparent redundancy of **whatever has no fins or scales in the water** is needed to include *all* water, since at first [:9] only seas and streams were mentioned. **[13] Of the fowl you will detest** The precise meaning of the word "you will detest" is slightly different here than in the phrase "Do not make yourselves detestable" [:43]. There, "yourselves" is the direct object of the verb. Regarding fowl, the meaning is: You should know that they are detestable, and you should think of them as detestable. ¶There is a bird whose name in Arabic is ***nesher***. This is evidence, as it were, that the same bird is meant here, since the two languages are related. **the *'ozniyya*** Although there is a single opinion that this bird is not found in inhabited regions [Ḥullin 62a], Sa'adya Gaon erred by translating it into the Arabic *al-'anka.* This Arabic word denotes a creature that does not exist anywhere in the world, and has never existed since Creation except as a fable — as their philologists will confirm. It is unlikely that GOD would forbid something that never

---

[1]This shows that the term "flesh" applies to fish. When our Sages excluded it in their discussion on vows [Ḥullin 104a], they were speaking of current usage.

the *peres*, and the *'ozniyya*; [14]the *da'a* and the *'ayya* including its kind; [15]every *'orev* including its kind; [16]the *bat-hayya'ana*, the *taḥmas*, the *shaḥaf*, and the *neṣ* including its kind; [17]the *kos*, the *shalakh*, and the *yanshuf*;

---

was. **[14] the *da'a*** Here, the word is a generic term that includes two species — the *da'a* and the *daya* [Deuteronomy 14:13] (compare, "but the birds he did not cut" [Genesis 15:10], where one term denotes both the turtle-dove and the young pigeon). The Exegetes were correct in identifying the *ra'a* [Deuteronomy 14:13] with the more specific meaning of *da'a* [Ḥullin 63a]. Thus Rabbi Yona ibn Janakh's argument (that it is unlikely that GOD would first say the general term [*ra'a*] and then say the specific term [*daya*]) disappears. ¶Some people say [Ḥullin 62b] that the word *nesher* [:13] comes from the word "I gaze at it" [Hebrew: *ashurennu*] [Numbers 24:17]; that *peres* [:13] comes from the word "spread" [Hebrew: *paros*] [Isaiah 58:7]; that *'ozniyya* [:13] comes from the word "strength" [Hebrew: *'oz*] with a superfluous *n*, and is identified with the *'akba*; that ***da'a*** comes from the word "will swoop" [Hebrew: *yid'eh*] [Deuteronomy 28:49]; that the ***'ayya*** is so called because it tends to dwell in certain islands [Hebrew: *iyyim*]; **[15]** and that ***'orev*** comes from the word "evening" [Hebrew: *'erev*] because it is known for its blackness [Song of Songs 5:11]. **[16] the *bat-hayya'ana*** [*feminine*] Some people say that the male of the species is rarely seen, like the cony [:6]. The existence of a plural form with a masculine suffix [Lamentations 4:3] is no proof that a male form exists. Many female nouns — "ewe" and "nanny-goat", for example — form their plural with a masculine suffix. **the *taḥmas*** from the word "plunder" [Hebrew: *ḥamas*]. **the *shaḥaf*** who causes tuberculosis [Hebrew: *shaḥeffet*]. **the *neṣ*** who has huge feathering [Hebrew: *noṣa*]; probably to be identified with a certain bird of the same name who flies South in search of a warm habitat [Job 39:26] **[17] the *kos*** as in, "the cache [Hebrew: *kos*] of the desert" [Psalms 102:7] — some say that this bird is *hidden* from the eye of man; i.e., it dwells in an uninhabited place **the *shalakh*** Some say that the nature of this bird is to throw away [Hebrew: *lehashlikh*] its young. ***yanshuf*** a bird who flies in darkness [Hebrew: *neshef*], because either the heat or the sunlight prevents it from appearing in daytime **[18] the *tinshemet*** Everyone who sees it is

[18]the *tinshemet*, the *qa'at*, and the *raḥam*; [19]the *ḥasida*,
the *'anafa* including its kind, the *dukhifat*, and the *'aṭallef*.
[20]All creeping beings that fly and that move on four legs
are a detestation to you. [21]However, these you may eat,
among the creeping things that fly and move on four legs:
those that have jointed legs above their forelegs with
which to jump from the ground. [22]These among them
you may eat: the *'arbeh*, including its kind, the *sal'am*, including its kind, the *ḥargol*, including its kind, and the
ḥagav, including its kind. [23]All creeping beings that fly,

---

terrified [Hebrew: *yashum*]. This name is also found among the insects [:30]. **the *qa'at*** Some people say that it is the nature of this bird to vomit [Hebrew: *lhaqi'*] its food. **the *raḥam*** Sa'adya Gaon asserts that the Arabic name of this bird is *rakam*, identical except for a *k* nstead of a *ḥ* (in their alphabet they use the same letter to denote both sounds). Others say that this bird is merciful [Hebrew: *meraḥem*] to its young. **[19] the *ḥasida*** This is the bird that appears at known times of the year [Jeremiah 8:7]. Some say that it disperses charity [Hebrew: *ḥesed*], but this is far-fetched. **the *'anafa*** who angers [Hebrew: *yit'annef*] quickly **the *dukhifat*** The Sadducees [a derogatory reference to Karaites — Translator] identify this bird with the chicken — what eternal fools! Who told them that? **the *'aṭallef*** a small bird that flies at night (the word is quadriliteral) **[20]** All small creeping beings that sometimes **fly** and sometimes **move on four legs** are a detestation. **[21]** This verse is spelled "with no jointed legs" but is traditionally read as **that have jointed legs**. The principal meaning is the latter. **to jump** This word has no cognate. Onkelos translated it into the Aramaic *lekappaṣa* (as in "leaps" [Hebrew: *mekappeṣ*] [Song of Songs 2:8]), meaning "skips"; and he translated correctly. **[22] *'arbeh*** so called because of its teemingness [Hebrew: *ribbuy*] **the *sal'am*** a species that alights on rocks [Hebrew: *sela'im*] **the *ḥargol*** if this word is quadriliteral, it has no cognate. If it is a compound of two words (like "that certain one" [Daniel 8:13]), then it means "leap-legged" [Hebrew: *ḥarag regel*] and its nature is opposite to the nature of the *sal'am*. **the *ḥagav*** This word is known from the Arabic. **[23] that have four legs** Scripture has already specified "that move on four legs" [:20];

and that have four legs are a detestation to you. [24]Through these will you become ritually impure: Whoever touches their remains will be ritually impure until the evening; [25]and whoever lifts their remains must immerse his clothes, but will be ritually impure until the evening. [26]All beasts that have hooves, but are not split, and who do not ruminate — they are ritually impure for you. Whoever touches them will be ritually impure. [27]All four-legged animals that move on their paws are impure for you. Whoever touches their remains will be ritually

---

but very probably there are creeping things that *have* four legs, but do not *walk* on them — they just fly. **[24] Through these you will become ritually impure** Some people say that the winged creeping beings [:32] and the birds that are to be detested [:13] are meant here. Others are of the opinion that **these** has the force of "the following", and that all four-legged animals that move on their paws [:27] are meant. I believe that **these** includes all the animals that have been mentioned above. **you will become ritually impure** The verb is in the reflexive [*hitpa'el*] form. Its *ṭet* is doubled to include the missing *tav*, like the *daled* in "he heard the Voice communing [Hebrew: *middabber*] with him" [Numbers 7:89] and "the one purifying himself" [14:8]. **will be ritually impure until the evening** Scripture employs brevity, not specifying that he first must immerse himself in water. **[25] whoever lifts** These laws are more severe than the laws of contact, as one must immerse one's clothes as well as one's body (this applies to all ritually impure animals). Here also Scripture employs brevity, **[26]** as it does when it here fails to specify the animals whose hooves are split but who do not ruminate, or the animals who ruminate but whose hooves are not split — though regarding both, Scripture has said, "do not touch their remains; they are ritually impure for you" [:8] **Whoever touches them** i.e., the abovementioned carcasses, becomes ritually impure in the manner mentioned above — until the evening. One Sadducee [a derogatory reference to a Karaite — Translator] heretic has read this verse to mean "Whoever touches them while alive becomes ritually impure". There is no need to answer words of lunacy. Scripture prohibited only their flesh, and specified, "do not

impure until the evening, [28]and whoever lifts their remains will immerse his clothes and will be ritually impure until the evening; they are ritually impure for you.

[29]These are ritually impure for you of the creeping beings that crawl on the ground: the *ḥoled*, the *'akhbar*, and the *ṣav* including its kind; [30]the *'anaqa*, the *koaḥ*, the *lṭa'a*, the *ḥomeṭ*, and the *tinshemet*. [31]These, of all the creeping beings are ritually impure for you. Whoever touches them when they are dead will be ritually impure until the evening. [32]Anything upon which a part of them falls, when they are dead, will be ritually impure — whether it be wooden, cloth, leather, sackcloth, or anything which may be used as a container — it will be brought into water and remain ritually impure until the evening, when it will be ritually pure. [33]If a part of them should fall inside any earthen vessel, everything in the

---

touch their *remains*" [:8]. **[27] that move on their paws** This verse contains the same law which was specified above [:24] regarding contact; **[28] and whoever lifts their remains** this is the same law which was specified above [:25] regarding lifting. This verse supports my explanation of the word "these" [:24], since there Scripture also says "whoever lifts their remains...". The two verses are found in the same paragraph and would otherwise be redundant. **they are impure for you** repeated to include all Israel — men, women, and children — within the scope of the law.

[29] We have no way of knowing what these eight creatures are (or the birds listed above) except through tradition. **These are impure for you** through contact **[31] These of all the creeping beings are ritually impure for you** These alone, among the ritually impure creeping things, will render other things ritually impure after they are dead. **impure until the evening** after having immersed himself **[32]** For the details of these laws, we rely on what has been handed down. **will be brought into water** the clothing or the sackcloth or

vessel will be ritually impure. You will shatter it. [34] Any edible food upon which water came will be ritually impure; any potable drink in the entire vessel will be ritually impure. [35] Anything upon which a part of their remains falls will be ritually impure. If it is an oven or a range, let it be broken: they are ritually impure; they shall be ritually impure to you. [36] However, a fountain or a ditch of gathered water is pure. Whatever touches their remains will be ritually impure. [37] If a part of their remains falls on a plantable, rooted plant, it is ritually pure. [38] Should water be placed on a plant, and then some of their remains falls upon it, it will be ritually impure for

---

the vessel that received the ritual impurity. **[33] if a part of them should fall** i.e., if a part of *any one* of them should fall (compare, "he was buried in the cities of Gil'ad" [Judges 12:7]) **[34] drink** [Hebrew: *mashqeh*] a noun; in the phrase "I used to *give drink*" [Hebrew: *mashqeh*] [Nehemiah 1:11] the same word is a verb. **[35]** Thus an oven for baking bread and a range for cooking meat are to be broken because they are ritually impure — for this is the decree of the King. **[36]** The Hebrew word for "well" is a feminine noun and denotes flowing water, as in "as a well keeps its water fresh" [Jeremiah 6:7]. A **ditch** is a cistern or a hole dug for collecting rainwater. Thus, a well is similar to a **fountain**. There was no need for the verse also to mention streams. The reasons Scripture speaks of **a ditch of gathered water** is that a ditch may also not have water. However, some say that the verse omits a connective, and that the verse should read "...a ditch, [or] gathered water..." (as in "Reuven [and] Shim'on" [Exodus 1:2], "the sun [and] moon" [Habakkuk 3:11]). **that touches their remains** the water that touches their remains will become ritually impure **[37] rooted** Either this is an adjective with a form similar to that of a participle, or it is an entirely different word and the verse specifies two things. Evidence for the latter is found in "and he gave them vegetables" [Daniel 1:16] where a similar word occurs. **[38] Should water be placed** While the field is being watered, one of their carcasses falls on the plant (some say: on the water). The word **placed** modifies

you.

[39]If one of the beasts that is yours to eat dies, whoever touches its flesh shall be ritually impure until the evening. [40]Whoever eats of its flesh will immerse his clothes and be ritually impure until the evening. Whoever lifts its flesh will immerse his clothes and be ritually impure until the evening. [41]All creeping beings that creep on the earth are a detestation: They will not be eaten. [42]All the creeping beings that creep on the earth — that move on the belly; that crawl on four legs, including the many-legged — you will not eat them for they are a detestation. [43]Do not defile yourselves through any creeping being, and do not make yourselves ritually impure and defiled by

---

the word **water** [*plural*], although its form is singular. Compare, "The water [*plural*] of separation was not thrown [*singular*] upon it" [Numbers 19:13]. **placed** this verb is in the *hof'al* form, like "brought" [Genesis 18:4].

[39] that is yours i.e., permissible to eat **shall be ritually impure until the evening** after he immerses in water **[40]** The laws of eating are severe, like the laws of carrying, for in fact both carry the carcass — one inside, and one outside. **[41] All creeping beings that creep on the earth** All creeping beings, including the eight mentioned above [:29], are mentioned again, to specify the prohibition against eating them. **[42] belly** as in "you will crawl upon your belly" [Genesis 3:14] **that crawl on four legs** here, denotes the tiny crawling things, as I have explained regarding the swarming things of the seas [*comment on* :10] **many-legged** an adjective formed from a noun in the construct case **[43] Do not defile yourselves** so as to become soiled and contaminated **do not make yourselves ritually impure** for it is known that the body which is eaten turns into the flesh of the body who eats it. **defiled** If this word is understood in sense of "defiled", then it is missing an *'alef* (like the word "from the beginning" [Deuteronomy 11:12]). Some say, though, that there are two different roots. The evidence for this assertion is the

eating them, [44]for I am GOD, your God. Sanctify yourself and you will be holy, as I am holy: Do not defile yourselves by eating any of the creeping beings that move on the ground. [45]For I am GOD who raised you up from the land of Egypt to be your God. Be holy for I am holy. [46]These are the laws concerning beasts, birds, all animals that move in water, and all animals that crawl on the ground: [47]To differentiate between the ritually impure and the ritually pure, between the animals that are eaten and the animals that will not be eaten."

[12:1]GOD told Moshe: [2]Tell the Children of Israel: "When a woman conceives and bears a male, she will become ritually impure for seven days; as in the days of separation

---

similar word "dumb" [Job 11:3], denoting a man who has no understanding. **[45] I am GOD** I raised you up out of the land of Egypt only in order to be your God. If you are not going to be holy, I will not be your God. Therefore, if it is your desire that I be your God, you must be holy. **Be holy for I am holy** therefore, I have told you "do not defile yourselves" [:43]. ¶The *vav* in Hebrew functions as a general-purpose connective particle, like the *f* of Arabic. Compare, "he left his laborers" [Exodus 9:21], and many others. **[47] To differentiate** among birds and creatures of the water **that are eaten** i.e., that are permissible for food **that will not be eaten** according to the Torah.

[12:2] When a woman conceives After completing the laws of ritually pure and ritually impure food, Scripture now discusses ritual impurity among people, beginning with the law of the new mother, because birth is a beginning. Many people claim that when a woman releases her egg before the man releases his sperm, she will give birth to a boy; and they cite this verse, pointing out "When a *woman* conceives...and gives birth to a boy". The sages of Greece are of this opinion – that the woman contains the seed, while the man's sperm is a congealing agent, and that children are congealed from the blood of the woman. **conceives** literally, "yields seed"

due to her indisposition, she will be impure. [3]On the eighth day the flesh of his foreskin must be cut off. [4]For thirty-three days she will remain in ritual purity of blood, but she must not touch hallowed foods, nor enter the Sanctuary until the end of her days of ritual purity. [5]If she bears a female, she will be ritually impure for two weeks, as in her separation. For sixty-six days she will re-

---

because in her reproductive function she resembles the Earth [Genesis 1:11]. ¶The *vav* of **she will become impure** is like the *f* of Arabic [*comment on* 11:45]. ¶The reason for her seven days of ritual impurity is that we wait for her to enter the next lunar quarter (we also find, in the course of an illness, that changes are seen after every seven days). **separation** a noun derived from an *'ayin-'ayin* verb, like "spoils" [Esther 9:15]. **her indisposition** similar in meaning to "sickness", as in "the ailments of Egypt" [Deuteronomy 7:15], because the menstrual blood is an unhealthy part of the woman's body **[3] on the eighth day** Our Sages have said [Megilla 20a]: on the *day*, and not at night. Thus a boy born a half hour before sunset can be circumcised six and a half days later — for a "day" in the Torah need not be a precise 24-hour period. **cut off** a verb in the passive [*nif'al*] form, probably an *'ayin-vav* verb (like "established" [Psalms 101:7]), derived from the word "circumcised" [Joshua 5:5]. Quite possibly, though, it is a *peh-nun* verb in the active [*qal*] form, derived from the word "circumcise" [Genesis 17:11]. The *nun* would disappear and be replaced by a doubling of the second consonant of the root (as in "swear" [Numbers 30:3]); Scripture has omitted the implied subject of the sentence — the boy's father, or the Court. **his foreskin** It is understood that the foreskin of his genital is meant, as there is no such thing as a foreskin of a heart [Deuteronomy 10:16], or a lip [Exodus 6:12], or an ear [Jeremiah 6:10] — these are all metaphors. **[4]** For a male child, GOD decreed the number of days required to complete his form in the womb. It has been clearly proven that a female child takes twice this amount of time. **she will not touch hallowed foods** even tithes, Teruma, and the meat of peace-offerings **the Sanctuary** the courtyard of the Tent of Assembly, or, in the times of the Temple, the Temple Court **in ritual purity of blood** or, "*with* ritual purity of blood" [:6] — both prepositions car-

main with the blood of her ritual purity. [6]At the end of her days of ritual purity for either a son or a daughter, she will bring a yearling lamb as a burnt-offering and a young pigeon or turtle-dove as a sin-offering — to the kohen, at the entrance of the Tent of Assembly. [7]He will sacrifice it before GOD. After he secures atonement for her, she will then have ritually purified her source of blood. This is the law for a woman who bears either a male or female. [8]If she cannot afford a lamb, she will bring two turtle-doves or two young pigeons, one as a burnt-offering and the other as a sin-offering. After the kohen makes an atonement for her, she will be ritually

---

ry the same meaning. **[5]** Although the *heh* of **her ritual purity** should be pronounced as a sign of the third person feminine singular, it is silent and imperceptible, like the *heh* in "he called her Novaḥ" [Numbers 32:42]. **the blood of her ritual purity** It is blood of ritual purity (in contrast to blood of separation) and it does not render ritually impure. **[6]** Were it not for the tradition, who would explain to us whether a **yearling** meant exactly one year old, or less than one year old, or greater than one year old [*cf. comment on* 23:12]? ¶Some people have suggested the reason for the burnt-offering of a lamb: perhaps, in her great distress, an evil thought entered her mind during childbirth. As for the sin-offering, perhaps she uttered it out loud. **[7] He will sacrifice** both the lamb and the young pigeon or turtle-dove. Scripture employs brevity and thus does not mention the breaking of the neck of the sin-offering bird (for the kohen does not eat of the sin-offering when it is a bird). **he will make atonement for her** as I have explained earlier **she will then have ritually purified her source of blood** This teaches us that after childbirth she does not become ritually pure until the end of the enumerated days. **[8] If she cannot afford a lamb** [literally: if a lamb cannot be found in her hand] A similar figure of speech is "he cannot afford" [literally: his hand cannot reach] [14:21]. **After the kohen makes an atonement for her, she will be ritually pure** This indicates that if the kohen does not make an atonement for her, she is not ritually pure. However, this ap-

pure."

[13:1]GOD told Moshe and Aaron: [2]Someone who has on his skin of his flesh a *ś'et* or *sappaḥat* or *baheret* — something of the *ṣara'at* disease on the skin of his flesh — let him be brought to Aaron the kohen, or to one of his descendants, the kohanim. [3]The kohen will see the spot on the skin of the flesh: If the hair of the spot has turned white and the appearance of the spot is deeper than the skin of his flesh, it is a symptom of *ṣara'at*: The kohen will

---

plies only inside the Holy Land.

[13:1] GOD told Moshe and Aaron Why Aaron? Because his pronouncements would determine, for all the afflicted of Israel, who shall be ritually pure and who shall be ritually impure. **[2] Someone** [Hebrew: *'adam*] Scripture did not use the other term for "man" — *'ish* (which denotes anyone of the House of Israel) — in order to include the foreigners. Compare, "any man among you who brings a sacrifice" [1:2]. In sacrifices there is one law for natives and aliens alike. Scripture also includes the foreigner in order that he should not render others ritually impure, since *ṣara'at* is a contagious disease. **let him be brought** willingly or unwillingly. Whoever notices any one of these symptoms may compel him to appear. **Aaron** denotes the High Priest, who will replace him **one of his descendents** denotes one of the ordinary kohanim, who can be found outside of the Temple, like the kohanim of 'Anatot [Jeremiah 1:1]. **the kohanim** excludes those who are unfit to serve **a *ś'et*** a kind of burn (compare: "beacon" [Judges 20:40]; "David burned them" [II Samuel 5:21]), whose derivation from the root *to lift* probably owes itself to the nature of fire, which is to be *lifted* upward. **a *sappaḥat*** from the words "reposit me" [I Samuel 2:36] and "they shall attach themselves" [Isaiah 14:1] — a disorder that *converges* on one place **[3] turned white** Here the verb "turned" is intransitive, and means the same thing as the passive form of the transitive (i.e., "has been turned"). **deeper** There is more pigment on the spot than on the skin ("deeper" here does not mean "lower"). **he will render him ritually impure** verbally, by declar-

examine it and render him ritually impure. [4]If he has on the skin of his flesh a white *baheret* that in appearance is not deeper than the skin, and whose hair has not turned white — the kohen will quarantine the symptom for a week. [5]The kohen will see it on the seventh day: If the symptom has not changed to his eyes, and the symptom has not spread on the skin — the kohen will quarantine him for a second week. [6]The kohen will see him on the second seventh day: If the symptom has dulled, and if the symptom has not spread on the skin — the kohen will purify him; it is a *mispaḥat*; he will immerse his clothes and become ritually pure. [7]If, after it was shown to the kohen for ritual purification, the *mispaḥat* spreads on the

---

ing that he is ritually impure **[4] a *baheret*** from "bright light" [Job 37:21]. This is known to be a telltale symptom. **the kohen will quarantine the symptom for a week** I.e., the person will be closed off. He will wait a week, for most illnesses change their course on the seventh day [*comment on* 12:1]. **[5] to his eyes** meaning, in appearance — as appearances are apprehended through the eyes. All the commentators have understood this locution to mean that the kohen who first saw the symptom must himself see no difference in its appearance. **spread** from "scattered" [Nahum 3:18]. **[6] second** a second time **dulled** Many scholars have said that this word means "darkened". Their evidence is the related word found in the phrase, "his eyes were too dim to see" [Genesis 27:1]. They said that the oxymoron "dark white" [:39] is similar to the phrase "white-red" [:19; :43] — i.e., that *both* pigments appear. But in my opinion, the word here means the opposite of **spread**, as in "his eyes had ceased to see" [Genesis 27:1]. A related word appears in the phrase "he did not restrain them" [I Samuel 3:13]. The apparent redundancy of **if the symptom has not spread** is understood to denote the appearance of symptoms elsewhere on the body. Thus there are two indicators:

1) the original symptom has receded; and
2) it has meanwhile not erupted in healthy skin.

the kohen will purify him i.e., he will declare that he is ritually

skin, it will be shown to the kohen a second time. [8]When the kohen sees that the *mispaḥat* has spread on the skin, he will render him impure: It is *ṣara'at*.

[9]If a symptom of *ṣara'at* occurs on a person and is brought to a kohen — [10]when the kohen sees a white *ś'et* on the skin, and it has changed to white hair, or if there is a growth of live flesh in the *ś'et* — [11]there is a long-standing *ṣara'at* in the skin of his flesh, and he will render him ritually impure. He must not quarantine him, for he is ritually impure. [12]If the *ṣara'at* develops on the skin until the *ṣara'at* covers the skin of the spot from head to foot, all according to the vision of the kohen's eyes — [13]the kohen will see that the *ṣara'at* has covered his entire skin, and he shall ritually purify the affliction: He has turned completely white; he is ritually pure. [14]On the day live flesh appears upon him, he will be ritually impure: [15]For the kohen, upon seeing the live flesh, will render it ritually impure. The live flesh is ritually impure; it is *ṣara'at*. [16]If the live flesh should revert and turn white, he must go to the kohen. [17]When the kohen

---

pure, since it was only a *mispaḥat*. However, **[7]** if it subsequently spreads, then he will be ritually impure.

[9] a person The Hebrew term *'adam* means the same here as it does above [:2]. **[10] changed** The implied object of the verb is the black hair, which was changed to white. **a growth** This denotes an area of **live flesh** — as opposed to a numb area, which would be called "dead flesh". **[11] long-standing** i.e., advanced **quarantine him** in Hebrew, a transitive verb with a direct and an indirect object, meaning to command another to close someone off **[13] he shall ritually purify the affliction** i.e., verbally, by declaring that he no longer renders others ritually impure. At this point the ailment has left him and has come out entirely to the surface. **[16] if**

sees that the symptom has turned white, he will render the symptom ritually pure; he is ritually pure.

[18]If one has an inflammation on the skin of his flesh and, in healing, [19]a white *s'et* or a white-and-red *baheret* will replace the inflammation — it will be shown to the kohen. [20]If the kohen sees that its appearance is lower than the skin and its hair turned white, the kohen will render him impure. It is a symptom of *ṣara'at* that has developed in the inflammation. [21]If, when the kohen sees it, there is no white hair therein and it is not deeper than the skin, and it is dull — the kohen will quarantine him for a week: [22]If it spreads on the skin, the kohen will render it ritually impure: It is a disease. [23]But if the *baheret* stays in its place, does not spread — it is the scar of the inflammation: The kohen will render him ritually pure.

---

it should revert i.e., it will probably revert.

[19] white-and-red intermediate between the two in appearance; or, part of it is white and part of it is red **[20] *ṣara'at*** an illness, as in, "I will send the *ṣir'a*" [Exodus 23:28].[1] **its appearance** Unlike ordinary words such as "her arm" and "her leg", this word does not have a *qamaṣ* under the *'alef* and an aspirated *heh* as a sign of the third person feminine singular possessive, because it comes from a *lamed-heh* root. **[21] when he sees it** [Hebrew: *yir'enna*] The *nun* is doubled here and in the word "he will quarantine him" [Hebrew: *yasgirennu*] [:11] to take the place of a missing pronomial *heh*, as in the words "from her" [Hebrew: *mimmenna*] and "from him" [Hebrew: *mimmennu*]. **[23] in its place** If it stayed in the same place (for there are diseases that are migratory) **the scar** from "all the faces shall be scorched by it" [Ezekiel 21:3], denoting a furnace, or

---

[1]Use of the verb "to send" does not imply that *ṣir'a* is a concrete noun. The same verb appears with abstract objects in "He sends out his word" [Psalms 147:18], "I will send a multitude of plagues" [Exodus 9:14], and "He sent upon them the fierceness of his anger" [Psalms 78:49].

[24]If the skin of one's flesh will have a burn caused by fire, and the scar of the burn will be a white-red or white *baheret*, [25]the kohen must see it: If the hair in the *baheret* has turned white, and its appearance is deeper than the skin, it is a *ṣara'at* that has developed in the burn. The kohen will render it ritually impure: It is a symptom of *ṣara'at*. [26]If, when the kohen sees it, there is no white hair in the *baheret* and it is not lower than his skin, and it is dull — the kohen will quarantine him for a week. [27]The kohen will see him on the seventh day: If it spreads on the skin the kohen will render him ritually impure: It is a symptom of *ṣara'at*. [28]But if the *baheret* stays in its place, it does not spread on the skin, and it is dull — it is a *s'et* due to the burn. The kohen will render him ritually pure, for it is the scar of the burn.

[29]If a man or a woman has an infection on the head or in the beard — [30]the kohen will see the infection: If its appearance is deeper than the skin, and it has thin golden hair, the kohen will render it ritually impure: It is a

---

heat, or fire.

[24] or white exclusively **[28] if the *baheret* stays in its place...and it is dull** I have already explained this last word [*comment on* :6]. This word is not used above, at the first mention of the *baheret*'s staying in one place [:23], because there the context implies that the *baheret* has not changed.

[29] Below, regarding baldness [:40], Scripture uses the specific term "man" [Hebrew: *'ish*] rather than the general term *'adam* in order to exclude women. Here, Scripture is obliged to specify **a man or a woman** because this verse discusses the beard; and otherwise, we might interpret both **on the head** and **in the beard** to apply only to men. **[30] golden** In Arabic this word denotes a near-

neteq; it is *ṣara'at* of the head or the beard. [31]If, when the kohen sees the *neteq*-infection, its appearance is not deeper than the skin, nor is there any black hair in it — the kohen will quarantine the *neteq*-infection for a week. [32]The kohen will see the symptom on the seventh day: If the *neteq* has not spread nor has golden hair in it, and the appearance of the *neteq* is not deeper than the skin — [33]he will shave; but the *neteq* he will not shave. The kohen will quarantine the *neteq* for a second week. [34]If, when the kohen sees the *neteq* on the seventh day, the *neteq* has not spread in the skin and its appearance is not deeper than the skin — the kohen will render him ritually pure: He shall wash his clothes and become ritually pure. [35]If the *neteq* spreads on his skin after his ritual purification, [36]the kohen will see it: If the *neteq* has spread on the skin, the kohen will not seek out golden hair: He is ritually impure. [37]If, to his eyes, the *neteq* has not changed, and black hair has grown in it: The *neteq* is healed; he is ritually pure and the kohen will render him ritually pure.

[38]If a man or a woman will have white stains on the skin of their flesh, [39]and the kohen will see that there are dull white stains on the skin of their flesh: It is *bohaq* that has

---

whitish color. **it is a *neteq*** from "as is broken a thread of tow" [Judges 16:9] denoting the evisceration of his hair **[33] he shall shave** his head, or his beard — but the area of the *neteq* will not be shaved. **[34] he shall wash his clothes** and there is no need to mention that he must immerse himself in water **[36] the kohen will not seek** meaning, "ask after" (as in "I seek them out" [Ezekiel 34:11]). This word also denotes the related concept "to discern" (as in "he will not distinguish between good and bad" [27:33]).

developed in the skin; it is ritually pure.

[40]A man whose head becomes bald — he is bald, he is ritually pure. [41]A man who loses the hair on the sides of his face — he is forehead-bald, he is ritually pure. [42]If a white-red spot appears in the baldness or in the forehead-baldness, it is a developing *ṣara'at* in his baldness or in his forehead-baldness. [43]When the kohen sees that there is a white-red *s'et* affliction in his baldness or in his forehead-baldness, like the appearance of *ṣara'at* of the skin of one's flesh — [44]he is a man afflicted with *ṣara'at*; he is ritually impure — the kohen will render him ritually impure; his infection is on his head. [45]He who has the infection of *ṣara'at*: His clothes will be rent; his hair must grow wild; his upper lip he shall cover; and he will cry

---

[39] it is *bohaq* This root is known from Rabbinic Hebrew [e.g., Sanhedrin 100a]; but it has no cognate in Scripture.

[40] his head all of it **becomes bald** As in, "I gave my cheeks to them that plucked off the hair" [Isaiah 50:6] (referring to the hair that surrounds the cheeks) **bald** from, "make no baldness on your head" [Deuteronomy 14:1] **[41] forehead-bald** This adjective has no cognates in Scripture outside of the current passage. In my opinion, it differs from "bald" [:40] in that the latter term denotes the upper part of the head. Scripture does not mention women here, because a woman's head does not become bald due to her excessive moisture (hair is a bit like grass in this respect). **[43] like the appearance of *ṣara'at* of the skin** i.e., like the appearance of *ṣara'at* elsewhere on the body **[45] his clothes shall be rent** (meaning, "torn"):

- He walks about differently, so that he can be recognized; or
- It is a sign of mourning. His clothes are to be torn, and his hair is to be uncut, because he is to mourn over his evil deeds which have brought him this disease.

out: "ritually impure, ritually impure." [46]All the while the infection is within him, he will be ritually impure. He is ritually impure: he must dwell alone; his dwelling must be outside the camp.

[47]If a garment has a symptom of *ṣara'at* in it — a woolen garment or a linen garment — [48]either in the warp or in the woof of the linen or the wool; or in a skin or in anything made from skin: [49]If the symptom is greenish or reddish on either the garment or the skin, whether in the warp or the woof, or in any leather utensil — it is a symptom of *ṣara'at*; it will be shown to the kohen. [50]When the kohen sees the symptom, he will quarantine the symptom for a week. [51]He must see the symptom on the seventh day. If the symptom has spread on the garment, either in the warp or in the woof, or in the leather — whatever utensil is made of the leather — the symptom is malig-

---

his upper lip denotes above the lip. The *mem* is part of the root (see, "he did not trim his mustache" [II Samuel 19:25]). **he shall cover** with his garments (from, "Who covers Himself with light" [Psalms 104:2]). The point is that he should not infect others with his breath. **[46] alone** I have already explained [*comment on* Lamentations 1:1] that the word is an invariant adverb.

[48] in the warp or in the woof The meanings of these two words are known. Probably **warp** [Hebrew: *sheti*] comes from the word "buttocks" [Hebrew: *shet*] [Isaiah 20:4] which contains its basic meaning. Evidence of this etymology appears in the phrase "when the foundations are destroyed" [Psalms 11:3]. **woof** [Hebrew: *'erev*] so called because it is interwoven [Hebrew: *yit'arev*] with the warp. **or in a skin** the skin itself **or in anything made from skin** e.g., a coverlet, or a waterskin **[49] greenish** [Hebrew: *yeraqraq*] from "vegetable" [Hebrew: *yereq*], which is likewise green in appearance. The suffix indicates a weaker color (as in "blackish" [Hebrew: *sheḥarḥoret*] [Song of Songs 1:6]) although some say

nant *ṣara'at*, it is ritually impure. [52]He must burn the garment, or the warp or woof of the wool or linen, or whatever leather utensil has the symptom; for it is malignant *ṣara'at*; it will be burnt in fire. [53]However, if the kohen sees that the spot has not spread on the garment, neither on the warp nor on the woof; nor on the leather utensil — [54]the kohen will command that they will launder that which has the symptom, and he will quarantine it for another week. [55]If the kohen will see the symptom after being laundered, and the symptom has not changed its appearance, nor has the symptom spread — it is ritually impure; you will burn it in fire: It has sunk into the reverse or into the obverse. [56]If, when the kohen sees it, the spot has dimmed after being laundered: He

---

the reverse. **[51] malignant** As in, "a pricking briar" [Ezekiel 28:24] — just as the "briar" is parallel to the "thorn", so the word "pricking" is parallel to the word "painful". The second *mem* in the word **malignant** is part of the root, thus it is not related to the word "disaster" [Deuteronomy 28:20]. The reason the passage does not mention silk, or cotton, is probably that:

- Scripture was speaking of materials that are commonly found. Likewise, Scripture says, "When you see your enemy's donkey..." [Exodus 23:5], although the law is the same for a horse or a mule.

or

- This disease rarely attacks anything other than wool or linen.

[55] being laundered a verbal noun in the passive, *hof'al* form **sunk** This word has no cognate in Scripture, but it is known from Rabbinic Hebrew to denote a diminution. It occurred in the **reverse** of the garment, or in its **obverse.**[1] **[57] if it reappear** [*feminine singu-*

---

[1]Sa'adya Gaon has explained that the word "reverse" [Hebrew: *qaraḥat*] denotes the other side, while the word "obverse" denotes the corners of the garment. If so, then the word "bald" [Hebrew: *qaraḥat* denotes the *back* of the head — a very appealing etymology.

will rip it out of the garment or the skin, whether from the warp or the woof. [57] If it reappear in the garment, whether in the warp or in the woof, or in any leather utensil — it is growing; burn whatever has the symptom on it in fire. [58] When you launder a garment, either the warp or the woof, or any leather utensil, and the symptom will go away from them — it will be washed a second time and will become ritually pure. [59] This is the law of the plague of *ṣara'at* of a garment of wool or linen, whether in the warp or in the woof, or of leather utensils — to declare it ritually pure or ritually impure.

[14:1] GOD told Moshe: [2] This will be the law of the *meṣora'* on the day of his ritual purification, when he will be brought toward the kohen. [3] The kohen will go outside the camp, and when the kohen will see that the affliction

---

lar] also **growing** [*feminine singular*] The abovementioned "malignancy" [*feminine singular*] is the subject of these two verbs. After having said "you will burn it" [:55], Scripture now explains that only the diseased spot must be burned. **[58] the spot having disappeared from them** The verb is in the past perfect tense, like many others which I have explained. **it will be immersed for a second time** The commandment is to immerse it twice. **immersed** a verb in the passive voice **[59] the law of the plague of *ṣara'at* of a garment of wool** Four consecutive nouns in the construct case! There is even, in Scripture, an instance of five: "men of valor for the work of the service of the house of God" [I Chronicles 9:13] — all dependent upon GOD, Who supports all who become dependent.

[14:1] Scripture says **GOD told...** to indicate the beginning of a new section, dealing with the laws of self-purification. **[2] he will be brought** connotes the same here as it does above [13:2; 13:9], since, once the affliction of *ṣara'at* has gone away, he might not want to bring the obligatory sacrifice. **[3] The kohen will go outside the camps** Although the kohen has declared him ritually pure, he still may not enter the camps (or the city) until he has offered

of *ṣara'at* has been cured of the person suffering *ṣara'at* [4]The kohen will command that he shall take, for the one purifying himself, two birds that are alive and ritually pure, a cedar stick, a bright woolen thread, and some hyssop. [5]The kohen will command to slaughter one of the

---

his ritual-purity sacrifice, and completed everything he has been commanded to do. **The kohen will go outside** This kohen is clearly not the High Priest, which clarifies my comment on "...or to one of his descendants, the kohanim" [13:2]. The grammarian Rabbi Yona ibn Janakh has said that **the affliction of *ṣara'at* has been cured of the person suffering *ṣara'at*** is backwards: Scripture should have said, "the person suffering *ṣara'at* has been cured of the affliction of ṣara'at". But why should we reverse the words of the living God on account of our limited understanding? Does not Scripture elsewhere say, "the *neteq* has been cured: he is ritually pure" [13:37] as well as "the affliction has been cured" [:48]? **[4] he shall take, for the one purifying himself** i.e., the kohen shall take it from the *other's* property (although one could also say that the person formerly afflicted with *ṣara'at* shall first give it to the kohen). In the word **the one purifying himself** the *tav* of the reflexive *hitpa'el* is absorbed into the doubling of the following *ṭet*; but the word is truly reflexive, as in "one who boasts" [Hebrew: *mit·hallel*] [Proverbs 25:14]. **two birds** All species of fowl are denoted by the term **birds**, and he may take any available fowl, so long as they are: **alive** i.e., not dead; and **ritually pure** — he may not take from the ritually impure species [11:13-19]. **a cedar stick...and some hyssop** These are the largest and the smallest of the species of plants, and we know this from the verse describing Shlomo's knowledge [I Kings 5:13]. (The word **hyssop** is known to us through tradition, and we do not need to investigate its meaning.) Thus the sufferer of *ṣara'at*, and the infected house [:49], and the ritual impurity of a corpse [Numbers 19:18], all resemble one another; and they all relate distantly to the Paschal sacrifice observed in Egypt [Exodus 12:22]. **[5] The kohen will command to slaughter** This command will be carried out by another kohen, or by an Israelite (some people say, the person who had suffered *ṣara'at* — but this is far-fetched). **toward an earthen vessel** i.e., *over* an earthen vessel. See also, "I have prayed toward this child"

**birds toward an earthen vessel containing running water.
[6]He will take the live bird, and the cedar stick, the
bright woolen thread, and the hyssop. He will immerse
them and the live bird in the blood of the bird slaughtered
over the running water. [7]He shall sprinkle seven times
upon the man purifying himself of *ṣara'at* and he will
render him ritually pure. He will send the live bird off
into the fields. [8]The purifiee shall launder his clothes.
He will shave off all his hair, wash with water, and then
become ritually pure. Afterwards, he will enter the camp;
but he will dwell outside his tent for a week. [9]On the
seventh day, he will shave off all his hair — that on his
head, his beard, and eyebrows — he will shave all his hair.
He will launder his clothes, wash his flesh in water, and
will become ritually pure. [10]On the eighth day he must
take two unblemished rams, and an unblemished ewe in**

[I Samuel 1:27]. **running water** i.e., water *taken from* a running source **[6] he will immerse them** i.e., the cedar, the hyssop, and the thread **over the water** with which the blood has been mixed **[7] he shall sprinkle** the diluted blood, after the immersion both of the live bird and of the abovementioned objects. He sprinkles with all three objects, or with the hyssop alone, as in the case of someone ritually impure through contact with a corpse [Numbers 19:18]. **into the fields** an uninhabited place, so that the *ṣara'at* does not spread **[8] he shall launder...he will shave off all his hair** Scripture does not specify when this will occur. **he shall wash with water and become ritually pure** in the evening, as prescribed. **[9]** Scripture subsequently explains that all this will take place after seven days (this was the reason for Miriam's [Numbers 12:15] seven-day confinement). Scripture also explains, when **he will shave off all his hair:** on the seventh day, that it includes **on his head, his beard, and eyebrows**[1] as well as **all his hair** — i.e., the hair on his legs, and, according to some, even the hair on his arms,

[1]This word is related to "the upper part" [Ezekiel 43:13]

its first year; three-tenths of fine flour for a cereal-offering mixed with oil, and one *log* of oil. [11]The kohen performing the purification will halt them, and the purifiee, before GOD, at the entrance of the Assembly Tent. [12]The kohen will take one of the rams and offer it as a guilt-offering together with the *log* of oil: He will wave them as a wave-offering before GOD. [13]He will slaughter the ram in the place where the sin- and the burnt-offerings are slaughtered, in a holy place; for the guilt-offering, like the sin-offering, is for the kohen — it is most hallowed. [14]The kohen will take some of the blood of the guilt-offering, and place it on the lobe of the purifiee's right ear, on the thumb of his right hand, and on the big toe of his right foot. [15]The kohen will take from the *log* of oil: He will pour some on the kohen's left palm. [16]The kohen will dip his right finger into the oil on his left palm, and

---

his thighs, and his chest **[10] two rams...and a ewe** Since the illness of *ṣara'at* is a rebuke for acts of the tongue, he must offer one ram as a burnt-offering, as prescribed for any emergent impulse [*comment on* 1:4]; one ram as a guilt-offering, following the rule for a guilt-offering [5:18]; and a female for a sin-offering, following the rule for a sin-offering [4:28]; and **three-tenths** in accordance with the principle of one-tenth per lamb [Numbers 15:4]. **one *log*** a unit of measurement. This word has no cognates, nor is its meaning evident. These particular rams and lambs (even the guilt-offering and the sin-offering) go exclusively to the officiating kohen, except for the suets which must be burnt. **[14]** He who purifies himself from a corporeal *ṣara'at* is like a kohen undergoing consecration [8:24]; for sin is like a spiritual *ṣara'at.* **lobe** This word's meaning is evident from context, and it symbolizes that one must attend to what has been commanded. **thumb** denotes the joint of the thumb, which is the origin of all activity **right** because of the greater strength of the right side **[15] on the kohen's left palm** the left palm of the kohen who is performing the ritual purification (as evident from the following verse). This repetition of the antecedent

will sprinkle some of the oil with his finger seven times before GOD. [17]From the remaining oil on his palm the kohen will place some on the lobe of the purifiee's ear, on the thumb of his right hand, and on the big toe of his right foot — upon the blood of the guilt-offering. [18]The remainder of the oil in the kohen's palm he will place on the purifiee's head. The kohen will secure atonement for him before GOD. [19]The kohen will sacrifice the sin-offering to atone for the man undergoing purification from his ritual impurity; then he will slaughter the burnt-offering. [20]The kohen will put the burnt-offering and the cereal-offering on the altar; the kohen will secure atonement for him, and he will be ritually pure.

[21]If he is poor and cannot afford, he will take for his atonement one ram as a guilt-offering to be waved; one-tenth of fine flour mixed with oil as a cereal-offering, a *log* of oil, [22]and two turtle-doves or two young pigeons, whichever he can afford: One will be a sin-offering, the other a burnt-offering. [23]He will bring them, on the

---

conforms to Hebrew usage. **[16] before GOD** i.e., toward the entrance of the Tent of Assembly **[17] upon** [the site of] **the blood of the guilt-offering** which is on the lobe and on the major digits **[19] the kohen will sacrifice the sin-offering** The female lamb will be brought as an ordinary sin-offering. **[20] will perform the burnt-offering** which consists of the male lamb, and its corresponding cereal-offering, one-tenth of an 'efa (some say that all of the cereal-offering should be brought with the burnt-offering). The guilt-offering is brought first, because it is the most important. **and he will be ritually pure** Only then does he become ritually pure like everybody else.

[21] poor This word can denote bodily ailments, as in "poor and malformed" [Genesis 41:19], "Happy is he who considers the poor" [Psalms 41:2], and "so lean, O son of the king" [II Samuel

eighth day of his ritual purity, to the kohen; to the outer entrance of the Tent of Assembly, before GOD. [24]The kohen will take the ram of guilt-offering and the *log* of oil, and the kohen will wave them as a wave-offering before GOD. [25]He will slaughter the ram of the guilt-offering, and the kohen will take some of the blood of the guilt-offering and place it on the lobe of the purifiee's right ear, and on the thumb of his right hand, and on the big toe of his right foot. [26]The kohen will pour some of the oil on the kohen's left palm. [27]With his right finger, the kohen will sprinkle some of the oil that is in his left palm seven times before GOD. [28]The kohen will place some of the oil that is in his palm on the lobe of the purifiee's right ear, on the thumb of his right hand, and on the big toe of his right foot — upon the place of the blood of the guilt-offering. [29]The remainder from the oil in the kohen's palm he will place on the purifiee's head to secure atonement for him before GOD. [30]He will sacrifice one of the turtle-doves or one of the young pigeons — whatever he can afford. [31]Of what he can afford, one of them will be a sin-offering and the other a burnt-offering with the cereal-offering. The Kohen will secure atonement for the purifiee before GOD. [32]This is the law for the person who has the disease of *ṣara‘at* who cannot afford his ritual purification.

[33]GOD told Moshe and Aaron, saying: [34]When you come to the land of Canaan, which I am giving you as a possession, and I will place a *ṣara‘at*-symptom in the house of

---

13:4]; and it can also denote lack of wealth.

[33] **GOD told Moshe and Aaron** This phrase introduces the

the land of your possession, [35]the possessor of the house will come and will tell the kohen, "Something like a symptom appears to me in the house." [36]The kohen will command and they will empty the house while the kohen has not yet come to see the symptom, so that everything in the house will not become ritually impure; afterwards the kohen will come to see the house. [37]If, when he sees the symptom, the symptom in the walls of the house is strong greenish or reddish, and they appear sunk into the wall — [38]the kohen will go out of the house to the entrance of the house. He will quarantine the house for a week. [39]The kohen will return on the seventh day. If he sees that the disease has spread on the walls of the house, [40]he will command and they will remove the stones that have the symptoms. They will throw them outside the

---

exposition on *ṣara'at* of a house. **[34] When you come to the land of Canaan** These laws apply only to the Holy Land, because of its great importance, insofar as the Holy Land contained the Temple, wherein resided the Glory. **I will place** These symptoms require Divine intervention. **[35] the possessor of the house will come** he is obliged to come to the kohen. **[36] they will empty the house** the owner of the house, as well as all the members of his household — use of the plural form emphasizes that they shall empty the house swiftly **while the kohen has not yet come** He will proceed to quarantine the house, because its status is in doubt; but while he has not yet come, they may act on the benefit of the doubt. **[37] strong** This word has no cognates. It is not known whether it is quadriliteral with a repeated final letter, or deṛived from a five-letter root. Its meaning must be inferred from context. Some people translate "symptoms", or "threads". Others maintain that it is a compound from sh-q-' (as in "the fire died down" [Numbers 11:2]) and r-r (as in "his flesh dribbles" [15:3]) — but this is far-fetched. **and they appear** Each one of them appears **sunk** [*singular*]. **[40] and they will remove the stones** The verb means "to remove", as in "remove me from the violent man" [Psalms 140:2].

city in a ritually impure place. [41]He will scrape the house around from inside, and they will pour the clay they scraped off in a ritually impure place outside the city. [42]They will take other stones and bring them to replace the stones, and he will take different clay and plaster the house. [43]If the disease return and develops in the house after the removal of the stones, and after scraping the house, and plastering — [44]the kohen will come. If he sees that the disease has spread in the house, it is a malignant *ṣara'at* of the house; it is ritually impure. [45]He will tear down the house: its stones, its wood and all the clay of the house. He will take it to a ritually impure place outside the city. [46]Whoever comes into the house all the while it is quarantined will be ritually impure until evening. [47]Whoever lies in the house will im-

---

in a ritually impure place so that they will be clearly recognized as ritually impure, and no one will take them **[41] scrape the house** from "chisels" [Isaiah 44:13] and also related to "cassia" [Psalms 45:9], which means "stripped". Some say that they shall scrape the affected region — but this is not correct, since the illness has already spread. Rather, they shall scrape everything, but remove the affected region alone. **[42] take** [*plural*] and **bring** [*plural*] Many people act in unison, quickly [*comment on* :36]. **will take** [*singular*] **different clay** The owner of the house will do this if he wishes to continue to live there. **plaster** the opposite of "scrape" [:41], from "they daub it with whitewash" [Ezekiel 13:10] **[43]** If the plague returns, the kohen will come **after the removal** i.e., after his having removed the stones, and after **scraping the house** previously. **[45] He will tear down the house** he will command others to tear it down. In the same sense, **he will take** means, he will command others to take. Most likely, the house had been quarantined for a second seven-day period, but Scripture employs brevity in not stating so explicitly. This is borne out by the phrase **[46] all the while it is quarantined** — both during the initial quarantine, and during the second quarantine **will be ritually impure until the evening** af-

merse his clothes; whoever eats in the house will immerse his clothes. [48]If the kohen comes and sees that the disease has not spread in the house after the plastering of the house, the kohen will render the house ritually pure, for the disease has been cured. [49]For the purification of the house, he will take two birds; and a cedar stick, a bright woolen thread, and hyssop. [50]He will slaughter one of the birds toward an earthen vessel containing running water. [51]He will take the cedar stick, the hyssop, the bright woolen thread, and the live bird, and he will immerse them in the blood of the slaughtered bird and in the running water He will sprinkle on the house seven times. [52]He will purify the house with the blood of the bird and the spring water; with the live bird, the cedar stick, the hyssop, and the bright woolen thread. [53]He will send the live bird outside the city to the fields. He will secure atonement for the house and it will be ritually pure. [54]This is the law for any *ṣara'at* affliction, or a *neteq*: [55] and for the *ṣara'at* of a garment, and of a house, [56] and for *s'et*, *sappaḥat*, or *baheret*; [57] to determine the day it is ritually impure and the day it is ritually pure. This is the law of *ṣara'at*.

---

ter having immersed himself, following the usual rule **[47] whoever lies** These laws are more stringent, hence he must **immerse his clothes**. He must also immerse himself, and he remains ritually impure until evening; but this is not explicitly restated, since anyone who lies or eats in the house also enters it. **[49] he will take** through an agent **[57] the day it is ritually impure** i.e., the day when a man, or a garment, or a house, becomes ritually impure or ritually pure

[15:1] *Ṣara'at* is a conspicuous disease. Scripture now explains the laws of those who are ritually impure from a *concealed* cause.

[15:1]GOD told Moshe and Aaron: [2]Tell the Children of Israel and say to them: Any man who will have a flow from his flesh — his flow is ritually impure. [3]This is the manner of his ritual impurity: If the flow from his flesh is saliva-like, or if it stops up his flesh from his flow, — it is his ritual impurity. [4]The man who flows renders ritually impure any couch upon which he lies; he renders ritually impure any article upon which he sits. [5]Someone who touches an article upon which he sat must launder his clothes, immerse in the water, and will be ritually impure until the evening. [6]Whoever sits on an object upon which the man who flows sat must launder his clothes, immerse in the water, and will be ritually impure until the evening. [7]Anyone who touches the flesh of the man suffering from a flow must launder his clothes, immerse in the water, and will be ritually impure until the evening. [8]If the man who flows should spit on a ritually pure person, he must launder his clothes, immerse in the water, and he

---

GOD told Moshe and Aaron Aaron is included because it is the kohanim who must distinguish between a woman who has a constant flow, and a menstruant (see the interpretation given by our Sages, of blessed memory, on the passage "a matter of blood" [Deuteronomy 17:8] [Sanhedrin 87a]). **[2] flow** as in, "flowing with milk" [Exodus 3:8] — i.e., trickling drops **from his flesh** a euphemism for the male genitalia **his flow** here, a noun **[3] This is the manner of his ritual impurity** to indicate the two different ways that the flow can occur **saliva-like** as in "he let his spittle run down his beard" [I Samuel 21:14] **or stops up** meaning "shut", from "it is sealed" [Isaiah 29:11]. This describes the situation when the flow thickens, and congeals, so that he can not ejaculate semen during sexual intercourse. **[4]** A single law applies to objects that were lain upon and objects that were sat upon; and everyone who touches any one of them is subject to the same law. **[7] anyone who touches the flesh of the man suffering from a flow** Here, the word "flesh" denotes *any* limb whatsoever [*cf. comment on* :2].

will be ritually impure until the evening. [9]Any riding seat upon which the man who flows rides is ritually impure. [10]Anyone who touches anything underneath it will become ritually impure until the evening; whoever lifts them must launder his clothes, immerse in the water, and will be ritually impure until the evening. [11]Whoever the man who flows touches — if he did not rinse his hands in water — will launder his clothes, immerse in the water, and will be ritually impure until the evening. [12]An earthen vessel touched by the man who flows will be shattered; all wooden vessels will be rinsed in water. [13]When the man suffering from a flow becomes ritually pure from his flow, he will count seven days of ritual purity. He will launder his clothes; he will wash his flesh in running water and become ritually pure. [14]On the eighth day he will

---

[8] If he spit an *'ayin-'ayin* verb (witness the doubling of the *qof* in "my spittle" [Job 7:19]). Even his spit is harmful, because the disease from which he suffers is contagious. Although people do not customarily spit in front of one another, it can nonetheless happen unintentionally: a man with a flow spits, and it falls on someone who was ritually pure. **[9] any riding seat** Provided that, in the opinion of the Exegetes, it can acquire ritual impurity **[10] anything underneath it** i.e., anything underneath the saddle transmits a weak ritual impurity. The ritual impurity acquired through carrying is more severe. **[11] if he did not rinse his hands in water** It would appear that if a man suffering a flow were to touch food (or any other object) with hands that had been rinsed, then the object should not become ritually impure, since it did not touch the area of the flow. However, we know [*Torat Kohanim* on this verse] that our ancestors all understood "hands" here to represent the entire body [and rinsing denotes immersion in a *miqveh* — Translator]; and we accept their words. Nevertheless, the *literal* meaning of the verse remains: Whenever a man suffering from a flow touches someone who is ritually pure — if his hands had been rinsed, then the person touched becomes ritually impure, but not his clothes; if his hands were unwashed, they also render one's clothes ritually

take for himself two turtle-doves or two young pigeons. He will come before GOD to the entrance of the Sanctuary, and give them to the kohen. [15]The kohen will sacrifice them — one as a sin-offering and one as a burnt-offering — and the kohen will secure atonement for him before GOD from his flow.

[16]A man from whom semen spills out must immerse all of his flesh in the water and will be ritually impure until the evening. [17]Any clothing or leather that has semen on it must be laundered in water, and will be ritually impure until the evening. [18]If a woman has sexual intercourse with a man, they will immerse in the water, and will be ritually impure until the evening.

[19]If a woman has a flow — blood will flow in her flesh — she will be separated for seven days. Whoever touches her will be ritually impure until the evening. [20]Whatever she lies upon during her separation will become ritually impure, and whatever she sits on will become ritually im-

---

impure. [13] **of ritual purity** i.e., from his first day of ritual purity [14] A burnt-offering and a sin-offering are given, because such a flow is an admonishment over sin.

[16] **a man from whom semen spills out** involuntarily **semen** as in, "a layer of dew" [Exodus 16:13] from "who can refill" [Job 38:37]. Those commentators err who explain **all of his flesh** as a reference to the male genitalia [*see comment on* :2]: their error lies in ignoring the word **all.** [17] It would appear that both one's skin and one's clothes require immersion if semen is found on them, whether the semen be wet or dry. However, the truth is in accordance with the received tradition [Nidda 54b]. [18] Having discussed matters that pertain to men, Scripture now turns to discuss matters that pertain to women.

pure. [21]Whoever touches what she lay on must launder his clothes, immerse in the water, and will be ritually impure until the evening. [22]Someone who touches any object upon which she sat must launder his clothes, immerse in the water, and will be ritually impure until the evening. [23]If he touched it through being on the seat, or on the object upon which she sat, he will be ritually impure until the evening. [24]If a man has sexual intercourse with her, her separation will be upon him, and he will be ritually impure for seven days; all couch upon which he lies will become ritually impure.

[25]If the flow of a woman's blood flows many days, outside of her period of separation, or if it flows in addition to her separation, all the days of the flow of her ritual impurity will be like the days of her separation: She will be ritually impure. [26]Any couch upon which she lies during all the

---

[19] **in her flesh** a euphemism for the female genitalia [23] **if on the seat** This refers to the abovementioned "utensil she sat upon" [:22]. The case is that of a utensil atop her seat, or a utensil atop another utensil. Thus, its ritual impurity is less severe. Scripture does not mention a saddle [*see* :9], because it speaks of things that are likely to occur; but the law in such a case would be the same. [24] **if a man has sexual intercourse with her** unintentionally (for example, if she began to menstruate while she was with him. It is in this sense that we understand the word **upon him**), since *karet* applies to the man who *intentionally* sleeps with a menstruant. The same law applies to a woman with a constant flow, although it is not explicitly mentioned. **all that he lies upon will become ritually impure** for he is ritually impure for seven days. Consequently, he can also render other people ritually impure, although this is not explicitly stated.

[25] **many days, outside of her period of separation** every woman has regular periods. This verse also describes a woman who

days of her flow will be to her like a couch of her separation; and whatever utensil she sits upon will be ritually impure like the ritual impurity of her separation. [27]Whoever touches them will become ritually impure. He must launder his clothes, immerse in the water, and will be ritually impure until the evening. [28]When she is ritually purified of her flow, she must count for herself seven days, and then she will be ritually pure. [29]On the eighth day she will take for herself two turtle-doves or two young pigeons; and she will bring them to the kohen at the entrance of the Tent of Assembly. [30]The kohen will sacrifice one of them as a sin-offering and one as a burnt-offering. The kohen will secure atonement for her before GOD for the flow of her ritual impurity. [31]You will keep the Children of Israel disassociated from their ritual impurity, so that they will not die in their ritual impurity by defiling My Sanctuary, which is in their midst. [32]This is the law for the man who flows, from whom semen comes out to become thereby ritually impure; [33]for her who is

---

suffers a constant flow immediately after her usual separation. **[29] and she will bring them** a very strange word, because it is stressed on the ultima **[31] you will keep disassociated** Some people explain that this word is missing a *heh*, and that it means "you will warn them". This, however, is unlikely, because a *heh* does not indicate diphthongs — only at the end of a word does it become silent or disappear. Rather, the word is related to "they will abstain from the sacrifices..." [22:2] and means, "you will distance them". The word "Nazirite" — one who distances himself from worldly desires — stems from the same root. This verb's form parallels that of "You shall divide [actually, "When you divide" — Translator] the land by lot" [Ezekiel 45:1]: the root *nun* disappears in the *dagesh*. **they will not die in their ritual impurity** i.e., they will not die *because* of their ritual impurity as a consequence of **defiling My Sanctuary**. **[32] to become thereby ritually impure** for it is obligatory that he remain ritually impure. I shall explain this later at

indisposed with her separation; for someone whose flow is a constant flow — for the man and for the woman; and for the man who lies with a ritually impure woman.

**[16:1]GOD spoke to Moshe after the death of the two sons
of Aaron, when they drew near before GOD and died.
[2] GOD said to Moshe: "Speak to your brother Aaron, and
let him not come at any moment into the Holiness beyond
the Partition; in front of the cover that is on the ark —
and he will not die, for I appear in the cloud upon the cover. [3]In this manner may Aaron enter into the Holiness:
with a bullock for a sin-offering and a ram for a burnt-**

---

greater length [*comment on* 19:31]. **[33] for the man** mentioned above, in "this is the law for the man suffering from a constant flow" [:32] **with a ritually impure woman** either a menstruant, or a woman suffering from a constant flow.

[16:1] after the death After warning Israel not to die [15:31], GOD now tells Moshe to warn Aaron not to die as his two sons died [10:2]. **they drew near** The *heh* at the end of this verbal noun (which appears in, "to approach the work" [Exodus 36:2]) here reverts to a *tav*, following the pattern for the feminine *heh.* Rabbi Abu al-Faraj Furqan ibn Asad erred when, in his system of thought, he classified the word as a noun. **[2]** This passage provides conclusive evidence that the children of Aaron offered the incense within the Partition. **into the Holiness** relative to the rest of the Tent of Assembly **in the cloud** They may enter only after making a cloud of incense, so that they do not see the Glory and thereby die — that is to say: I shall not be seen by you, except **in the cloud**. Others explain the phrase to mean, "because I dwell **in the cloud** which is **upon the ark-cover**", in the sense of "GOD said that he would dwell in the thick darkness" [I Kings 8:12]. **[3] with a bullock** This does not mean that he should bring the bullock into the Holy of Holies. Rather, it means that he must first sacrifice his own bullock as a sin-offering, to atone for himself and for the kohanim (some say that his bullock also atones for the Levites, be-

offering. [4]He will wear a consecrated linen tunic, and short linen trousers will be on his flesh; he will gird himself with a linen belt, and hat himself with a linen turban; they are consecrated garments — he will immerse in the water, and don them. [5]From the community of the Children of Israel, he will take two he-goats for a sin-offering, and one ram as a burnt-offering. [6]Aaron will offer the bullock sin-offering that is his; he will make atonement for himself and for his household. [7]He will take the two he-goats and stand them up before GOD at the entrance of the Tent of Assembly. [8]Aaron will place lots on the two he-goats; on one lot: FOR GOD, and on one

---

cause they came across the verse "You will inscribe Aaron's name upon the rod of the Levite tribe" [Numbers 17:18] — but this is far-fetched; the Levites are reckoned with the rest of Israel). **[4] a consecrated linen tunic** This verse does not mention the breastplate, or the ephod, or its robe, since they are already mentioned in the passage that ends in the verse "its sound shall be heard when he enters the holy place...." [Exodus 28:35]. However, the men of the Second Temple did learn from this verse that the High Priest may officiate without the 'Urim and the Tummim (moreover, there were prophets then to take their place). **[6] Aaron will offer the bullock sin-offering** toward the entrance to the Tent of Assembly, as the usual manner. **make atonement for himself** After he slaughters it, he atones thereby for himself and for his family (some say that merely designating the bullock constitutes atonement). **[8] lots** These objects are known to us through the tradition which we have received from our ancestors. Sa'adya Gaon said that **'Azazel** is the name of a mountain, so called because it is mighty [Hebrew: *'az*]. A divine name [Hebrew: *'el*, powerful] appears as a suffix, in the sense of "the great mountains" [Psalms 36:7] and "Yequti'el" [literally, "hope in the Mighty One"] [I Chronicles 4:18]. The Gaon Halevy[1] held that the word **'Azazel** does not

---

[1][The identity of this scholar is uncertain, but is probably either Gaon Mevasser ben Kahana Kimai or Gaon Shmu'el ben Ḥofni — Translator]

lot: TO 'AZAZEL. [9]Aaron will offer the he-goat on which the lot FOR GOD fell, and he will sacrifice it as a sin-offering. [10]The he-goat on which the lot TO 'AZAZEL fell will be stood up before GOD, to make atonement on it; sending it to 'Azazel, toward the wilderness. [11]Aaron shall offer the bullock sin-offering that is his to secure atonement for himself and for his household: He will

---

contain such a suffix, because its *'alef* appears between two *zayin*'s. Some say that this mountain is near Mount Sinai, and that GOD commanded us to lead the goat up the mountain and to slaughter it there. Afterward, during the time of the Second Temple, the goat used to be led to a different mountain. The evidence that the particulars were reinterpreted is the otherwise superfluous verse "Aaron did everything..." [8:36]. In my opinion the festival of Shavu'ot was treated similarly, as I shall explain in its place [*comment on* 23:11]. One commentator has pointed out that the service in the Second Temple differed from the service in the First Temple: the High Priest lacked certain garments, and there was no ark-cover. He suggested that, originally, the scapegoat was sent into the *wilderness*, for so it is written: "he will send the goat into the desert" [:22]. The purpose is the same as that of the bird send "into the fields" [14:7] — an uninhabited place — in the case of someone purifying himself from *ṣara'at*. As conclusive evidence, he cites the phrase "to a barren region" [:22]. We may rebut this argument thus: The goat is first sent into the wilderness, as it is written. It is then pursued until it flees atop a high rock — at which point, in the words of our Sages, "he pushes it from behind" [Yoma 67a]. **[9] he will sacrifice it as a sin-offering** i.e., he will designate it for slaughter. Gaon Shmu'el ben Ḥofni HaKohen has said that, although the sin-offering goat is marked **for GOD**, the scapegoat is also for GOD. Scripture does not require his explanation, though, because the scapegoat is not a *sacrifice*, since it is not slaughtered. **[10] will be stood up** a verb in the passive, *hof'al* form. Normally the *yod* would be vocalized with a *qubbuṣ*; but the subsequent guttural letter causes the vowel to be lengthened to a *qamaṣ qaṭan*. Compare "all his substance shall be forfeited" [Ezra 10:8]. **to make atonement on it** through it, atonement will occur — and this will be accomplished by **sending it**

slaughter the bullock sin-offering that is his. [12]He will take the pan full of hot coals from the altar before GOD and fistsful of thinly-ground fragrant incense. He will bring this within the Partition. [13]He will put the incense on the fire before GOD, and the cloud of incense will conceal the cover which is over the Testimony, that he not die. [14]He will take some of the bullock's blood and sprinkle with his finger upon the ark-cover, eastward; he will sprinkle some of the blood seven times in front of the ark-cover with his finger. [15]He will slaughter the he-goat sin-offering that belongs to the people, and bring its blood into beyond the Partition; he will do with its blood as he did with the bullock's blood: he will sprinkle it upon the ark-cover and in front of the ark-cover: [16]He will secure atonement for the Holiness from the ritual impurities of the Children of Israel, and from their sins — all of their shortcomings. So will he do to the Tent of Assembly,

---

away. [11] After digressing somewhat on the subject of the goats, Scripture continues where it left off. **Aaron will offer** After bringing the bullock and the two goats to the Tent of Assembly, he begins by slaughtering his bullock. [12] **the pan** the one which had been designated **fistsful** both fists **fragrant incense** of the type already specified [Exodus 30:35] [14] We might think that the phrases **upon the ark-cover** and **in front of the ark-cover** are to be understood literally. However, the Exegetes have said [Yoma 52b; Yoma 54a] that **upon the ark-cover** means "between the poles"; while the true meaning of **in front of the ark-cover** is known only from their words [Yoma 55a]. [15] **He will slaughter the he-goat sin-offering that belongs to the people** Only now does he slaughter it, after emerging from the Holy of Holies — though some have incorrectly claimed that he slaughters it before the bullock [*comment on* :9]. [16] **he will perform atonement for the holiness** i.e., for the Holy of Holies **atonement** The blood will serve as a ransom, so that he not be destroyed on account of the ritual impurity of others. **So will he do for the Tent of Assembly** i.e., he will sprinkle seven

which dwells with them, among their ritual impurity. [17]No person shall be in the Tent of Assembly when he enters to make atonement within the Holiness, until he leaves; he will perform atonement for himself and for his household and for the entire community of Israel. [18]He will go out to the altar that is before GOD and perform atonement upon it. He will take some of the bullock's blood and some of the he-goat's blood and put it on the corners of the altar all around. [19]He will sprinkle some of the blood on it with his finger seven times; he will render it ritually pure, and consecrate it, from the ritual impurities of the Children of Israel. [20]When he finishes atoning for the Holiness, the Tent of Assembly, and the altar — he will offer the live he-goat. [21]Aaron will rest both his hands on the live he-goat's head; he will confess on it all the transgressions of the Children of Israel, and all their sins — every shortcoming. He will put them on the head of the he-goat and he will send it with a desig-

---

times before the ark-cover and on the corners of the incense altar **[17] no person** among the kohanim **to make atonement within the holiness** i.e., inside the Holy of Holies **he will perform atonement for himself and for his household** through his bullock sin-offering **and for the entire community of Israel** through their ram sin-offering **[18] he will go out to the altar** This denotes the sacrificial altar [according to *halakha*, it denotes the incense altar — Translator]. **[21] he will put them** After they depart from Israel, it is as if they are given over onto the head of the goat, and they go to a place where they will never more be noticed. Scripture speaks this way so that everyone can understand it. **designated** [literally: for the moment] someone who had been prepared for this moment (or, someone accustomed to go at any moment on Yom Kippur). The *yod* forms an adjective from the noun "moment", as in the adjective "inner" [I Kings 6:27]. Those people who translate the word as "well-informed" are wrong, in my opinion. Our Sages, whose words are true, said [Yoma 66a] that this person was a ko-

nated man into the wilderness; [22]and the he-goat will carry all their transgressions upon itself to a barren land. He will send the he-goat into the wilderness. [23]Aaron will enter the Tent of Assembly. He will remove the linen garments he wore when he went into the Holiness, and he will cache them there. [24]He will immerse his flesh in the water, in a holy place, and he will don his garments. He will go out and sacrifice his burnt-offering and the people's burnt-offering, securing atonement for himself and for the people. [25]He will kindle the suet of the sin-offering on the altar. [26]The man who sent the he-goat to 'Azazel will launder his clothes and he will immerse himself in water. Afterwards, he will enter the camp. [27]The bullock sin-offering and the he-goat sin-offering whose blood was brought to secure atonement into the Holiness — he will take out beyond the camp. They will burn in fire their hides, flesh, and dung. [28]Whoever burns them will launder his clothes and immerse his flesh in the water; af-

---

hen. **[24] in a holy place** in the courtyard of the Tent of Assembly (they used to raise a screen so he could undress). **his garments** which he wears every day (but some people assert that these **garments** are the ones mentioned in the previous verse; and as evidence they cite the absence of the phrase "he will put on other garments" [6:4]). **his burnt-offering** his ram **the people's burnt-offering** This includes the people's ram, and their bullock, and their seven lambs, for so it is written [Numbers 29:8]. **[25] the suet of the sin-offering**:

1) the suet of the bullock sin-offering [:11]
2) the suet of the goat sin-offering [:15]
3) the suet of the kid sin-offering (an ordinary kohen's offering which is not entirely burned, as described in the *parasha* of *Pinḥas* [Numbers 29:11])

[26] he will immerse himself in water This is sufficient, as he is *not* ritually impure until evening. **[27] he will take out** i.e., he will tell an agent to do it **They will burn** The kohanim will burn it, and

terwards, he will enter the camp. [29] It will be an everlasting decree for you: In the seventh month, on the tenth of the month, you will afflict your souls and you will not do any labor — both the native, and the convert who dwells amid you; [30] for on this day he performs atonement for you, to render you ritually pure. From all your sins you will become ritually pure before GOD. [31] It is a Sabbath of Sabbath to you; you will afflict your souls; this is an

---

[28] each of them will immerse himself in water, and immediately return to the camp. The fact that Scripture says **he will enter the camp** is evidence that their return was immediate — otherwise, what point is there in mentioning it? **[29] It will be an everlasting decree for you** i.e., this sacrificial service **in the seventh month, on the tenth of the month, you will afflict your souls** From the passage "let your soul delight in fatness" [Isaiah 55:2] we know that "affliction" of a soul must be the opposite of its delight — i.e., a fast. Moreover, the phrase "be generous to the hungry" [Isaiah 58:10] means the same as "satisfy the afflicted soul" [Isaiah 58:10], because the prophetic style is to speak in parallelisms. Since we possess a tradition for the meaning of this idiom, there is no need to adduce additional evidence (the phrase "I afflicted my soul with fasting" [Psalms 35:13] does *not* provide additional evidence, because there the word "fasting" is explicitly mentioned). The general rule is: "affliction of soul" denotes fasting, wherever it appears in Scripture. **the native, and the convert who dwells amid you** We do not allow him to work, but we do not exclude him on account of the fast. **[30] performs atonement** The High Priest shall perform atonement for you. Regarding the scapegoat, the Exegetes have said that the phrase "will be stood up alive...to make atonement" [:10] means that the kohen performs atonement in the act of standing it up. **from all your sins** As I have explained, [*comment on* Exodus 34:6], the noun "sin" is a general category. You will find it used to denote both unintentional acts [Deuteronomy 19:15] and intentional thoughts [Isaiah 30:1]. **[31] a Sabbath of Sabbath** Some say that this phrase means, "a Sabbath for the spirit, and a Sabbath for the body". Others interpret in the sense of "the Sabbath of all Sabbaths" — i.e., the loftiest of all Sabbaths. It is also plausible

everlasting decree. [32] The kohen who has been anointed and installed to serve instead of his father will perform atonement; wearing the linen garments, the consecrated garments, [33] he will perform atonement for the holy sanctuary; he will perform atonement for the Tent of Assembly and for the altar; he will perform atonement for the kohanim and for the entire people — the community. [34] This will be for you an everlasting decree: to perform atonement for the Children of Israel for all their sins once a year." He did what GOD commanded Moshe.

[17:1] GOD told Moshe: [2] Tell Aaron and his sons and all the Children of Israel, say to them: This is the thing that GOD commanded: [3] "Any man of the House of Israel who slaughters a bull, a ram, or a goat in the camp, or who slaughters it outside of the camp, [4] but he does not bring it to the entrance of the Tent of Assembly to offer it as an offering to GOD, before GOD's Sanctuary — blood will be

---

that the two words are synonyms, and that they often appear one after another [*see* Exodus 16:23] **an everlasting decree** to fast **[32] the kohen will perform atonement** Scripture now returns to the previous discussion, explaining over what the kohen performs atonement. **anointed** the one who is anointed with the anointing-oil, after being consecrated **wearing** the one who wears these holy garments — for no one else may wear them **[33] the holy sanctuary** the area inside the Partition **he will perform atonement for the kohanim and for the entire people — the community** The Levites are included in the latter category, because they are not kohanim (although every kohen is a Levite, not every Levite is a kohen). **[34] this will be for you...** This has been said before [:29], but is here repeated to add the phrase **once a year**. **He did** i.e., Aaron did.

[17:2] Tell Aaron and his sons for they constitute Israel's ritual slaughterers. **[3]** If Scripture had *only* said **in the camp**, it would

reckoned to that man, as if he had spilled blood. That man will be cut out from amid his people. [5] In order that the Children of Israel will bring their sacrifices, which they sacrifice on the open field — that they bring them to GOD, to the kohen at the entrance of the Sanctuary. They will sacrifice them as peace-offerings to GOD. [6] The kohen will throw the blood on GOD's altar at the entrance of the Tent of Assembly and he will kindle the suet that it be willingly acceptable to GOD. [7] They will then no longer sacrifice their sacrifices to the satyrs after which they stray." This will be an everlasting decree for them throughout their generations. [8] Say to them: "Any man of the House of Israel or of the resident aliens who live in

---

be permissible to slaughter animals anywhere outside of the camp. [4] The commandment that is herein given also applies to the Temple; but there it covers only the districts close to Jerusalem (the definition of "close" is known from tradition [Qiddushin 57b]). In faraway places one may simply slaughter the animal and eat its flesh (for so it is written [Deuteronomy 12:21]). Many people have incorrectly said that, during the Exile, *all* flesh is forbidden. They assert that the passage "nor did meat or wine come into my mouth" [Daniel 10:3] denotes an additional abstinence from the flesh of fish. I do not wish to spend time refuting them. [5] **In order that the Children of Israel will bring** This is the reason for the commandment. The meaning of **on the open field** is given in the subsequent verse, "They will then stop..." [:7]. [7] **to the satyrs** [Hebrew: *laśśe'irim*] hese are the demons, so called because when one sees them, one's body convulses [Hebrew: *yiśta'er*]. Also, the lunatics who see these demons experience visions of goat-like creatures [Hebrew: *śe'irim*]. The word **no longer** teaches that, in Egypt, this *had* been Israel's practice. **they stray** [literally: they prostitute themselves] Anyone who summons demons, or believes in them, is faithless to his God. He thinks that benefit or harm can come from a source other than GOD, the Glorious and Awesome. This passage does not mention the resident alien, because it pertains to Israel's sacrificial offerings; however, the subsequent pas-

their midst, who will offer a burnt-offering or a sacrifice,
[9]but will not bring it to the entrance of the Tent of Assembly to sacrifice it to GOD — that man shall be cut off
from his people. [10]Any man of the House of Israel or of
the resident aliens living in their midst who will eat any
blood — I will direct My Face against the person who eats
the blood and will cut him out from amid his people.
[11]For the life of the body depends on the blood. I have
given it to you for the Altar, to atone for your lives, because the blood atones with the soul. [12]I therefore say to
the Children of Israel: No one among you will eat blood;
the resident alien who dwells in your midst will not eat
blood. [13]Any man of the Children of Israel or of the
resident aliens dwelling in their midst who will capture a
game animal or a bird that may be eaten — he will spill

---

sage [8] *does* mention the resident alien. Here the resident alien is mentioned because Israel must not allow an alien to offer idolatrous sacrifices within the Land of Israel. Likewise, [10] they may not drink blood, which is forbidden [11] because it represents life: **the life of the body depends on the blood** (A man lives by means of the blood which comes from his heart.) **atones with the soul** The blood secures atonement by means of the animal spirit which it formerly contained (in the sense of "a soul for a soul" [Exodus 21:23]). Other people interpret **atones with the soul** as a reference to the human soul, as in, **to atone for your lives** [literally: for your souls]. This interpretation is senseless, because it would make the verse redundant. [13] **a game animal** like a deer or a gazelle **or a bird that may be eaten** We learn from this verse that we also may not permit a resident alien to eat pork, or horseflesh, or a bird of prey[1] in the land of Israel. ¶We are commanded not to eat blood [:10]. When we slaughter an animal fit to be sacrificed, we are further commanded to spill its blood on the Altar only [:4], and nowhere else. Consequently, GOD commanded us to conceal the

---

[1]All birds of prey are ritually impure [Ḥullin 59a].

its blood and cover it with dust. [14]For the life of all flesh — its life depends on its blood. Therefore I say to the Children of Israel: Do not eat the blood of any flesh, for the life of any flesh is its blood; whoever eats it will be cut off. [15]Whoever eats the carcass of an animal that has died on its own, or of an animal that has been torn by wild beasts, both the native and the stranger, will launder his clothes and immerse in the water. He will be ritually impure until the evening; then he will be ritually pure. [16]If he does not launder, or wash his flesh, he will bear

---

blood of any slaughtered animal which is *not* offered as a sacrifice — probably so that no one might see the blood of a deer, or a gazelle, or a bird, and mistakenly think that it was a sacrifice to a foreign god. In the *parasha* of *R'eh* I shall explain a more profound meaning to this verse [*comment on* Deuteronomy 12:25]. **[14] its life depends on its blood** The blood is bound up with the breath of life (it is well known that there are two categories of veins coming out of the left side of the heart: those that carry blood, and those that carry the breath), as the olive oil in an oil lamp is bound up with the fire. **therefore I say** i.e., therefore I *have said*, in the current passage. ¶After mentioning wild animals, and birds, which are not sacrificed, **[15]** Scripture now mentions **Whoever eats the carcass of an animal that has died on its own, or of an animal that has been torn by wild beasts** — because such flesh is also not sacrificed (Another reason for juxtaposing these two passages is that the previous passage mentions hunting). Someone who *intentionally* eats such flesh violates a negative commandment, and incurs corporal punishment; if he *unintentionally* eats it, he must bring a sin-offering. **the stranger** Here an objection can be raised: Does not Scripture elsewhere assert, "you may give it to the stranger who is within your gates, and he may eat it" [Deuteronomy 14:21]? The answer is that there the resident alien is meant; this verse, on the other hand, describes "the stranger who dwells among you" [16:29] — i.e., a proselyte. We must not allow a proselyte to eat an animal that has died on its own; but we may give it to a resident alien passing through our gates, for him to eat it outside. **[16] he will bear his iniquity** forever — until his iniquity is forgiven through

his iniquity."

[18:1]GOD told Moshe: [2]Tell the Children of Israel, say to them: "I am GOD your God. [3]Do not practice the deeds of the land of Egypt, wherein you dwelt; do not practice the deeds of the land of Canaan, whither I bring you; do not follow their customs. [4]Practice My judgments, and observe My statutes, to go therein; I am GOD, your God. [5]Observe My statutes and My laws — someone who practices them will live by them. I am GOD.

[6]Anyone with his near kin — do not come close and re-

---

the punishments which GOD will bring upon him. ¶Because the current passage deals with demon-worship — an Egyptian practice — it is attached to the upcoming passage on incest — a Canaanite practice (this is borne out by the explanation given at the end of that passage [18:27]).

[18:2] I am GOD your God here means: Only on the following conditions will I be your God. **[3] the deeds of the land of Egypt** denotes the Egyptian legal system (as we see from the subsequent phrase, "Practice *My* judgments" [:4] — referring to the judgments that GOD promulgated in the Book of the Covenant, which is detailed in the *parasha* of *Mishpaṭim* [Exodus 24:7]). **Do not follow their customs** One must not develop a habit of behaving their way, until he ultimately becomes accustomed to it. **[4] I am GOD your God** i.e., only then will I be your God **[5]** This verse explains that **My statutes and My laws** bring life to those who practice them — life in this world, and life in the World to Come. Whoever grasps the inner meaning of GOD's laws will enjoy eternal life, and never die. Accordingly, the verse concludes with **I am GOD**, as I have explained [*comment on* Exodus 6:3].

[6] anyone without exception. Since the verse does not mention "of the House of Israel" [e.g., 17:3], we must not allow a resident alien to perform any of these enumerated abominations in

veal nakedness: I am GOD.

[7]Do not reveal your father's nakedness or your mother's nakedness; she is your mother, do not reveal her nakedness.

[8]Do not reveal your father's wife's nakedness; she is your father's nakedness.

[9]Your sister's nakedness – your father's daughter, or

---

our land. He may not pollute our land [*see* Numbers 35:34]. **do not come close** a euphemism for sexual intercourse, as in "I came near to the prophetess" [Isaiah 8:3] (compare the related euphemism, "do not approach women" [Exodus 19:15]). **with his near kin** This term denotes incest in general. Afterward, its particulars will be listed (HaRav Aaron ben Yosef Sargado HaKohen said that the apparent redundancy of this verse is needed to exclude "wasting of seed" from the incest prohibition). **nakedness** something indecent, something which must be covered if it is laid bare **I am GOD** GOD loves someone who withdraws from the world in order to serve Him and to understand His words (for example, men and women had to separate from one another three days before the revelation at Sinai). This mystery applied to the very first man [*comment on* Genesis 1:6] and is intrinsic to the human condition. Since human impulses are animalistic by nature, it was not feasible to forbid *all* women; but He did forbid all those with whom one is constantly in contact (In the *parasha* of *Ki Teṣeh* I shall further reveal a deep and hidden mystery [*comment on* Deuteronomy 23:10]). The phrase **I am GOD** suggests that by dirtying oneself carnally, one distances himself from the Holy and Revealed Name.

[7] **your father** Scripture begins with the father (because the father precedes the son), and forbids a son from having relations with anyone who is a near kin of his father or mother. This primarily denotes his mother, and

[8] secondarily denotes his father's wife even if she is not his

your mother's daughter; born of the house, or born outside — do not reveal their nakedness.

[10]The nakedness of your son's daughter, or of your daughter's daughter — do not reveal their nakedness; for they are your nakedness.

[11]Your father's wife's daughter's nakedness — she who is sired by your father is your sister; do not reveal her

---

mother. Afterward,

[9] Scripture lists his sister, whether she is his father's daughter or his mother's daughter. **born of the house** i.e., born according to the ways of the House of Israel: after betrothal and wedlock. **born outside** i.e., born outside of wedlock. Other people interpret **born** in the sense of "were brought up under Joseph's guidance" [Genesis 50:23] — she is forbidden to you whether she grew up with you in the same house, or whether she lived in a different town or country and grew up **outside** of your father's house.

[10] Scripture then proceeds to mention his granddaughter.

[11] **your father's wife's daughter's nakedness** Some people say that this denotes a full sister, who is both his father's daughter and his mother's daughter. We consequently infer that whoever has relations with a full sister violates *two* prohibitions. Others assert that this verse merely strengthens the existing prohibition.[1] Probably the phrase **your father's wife's daughter** denotes a

[1]The Sadducees [a derogatory reference to Karaites — Translator] said that this verse does not denote his mother's daughter. They interpret the qualifier **born of your father** to mean that his father *raised* her. The case involves a father who married a woman who already had a small child. They explain the case of Tamar [II Samuel 13:1] similarly. Their evidence is the phrase "for he will not withhold me from you" [II Samuel 13:13] which shows that David did *not* raise her. Since the Exegetes have said that it is permitted to marry one's stepsister [Soṭa 43b], there is no need to reply to these fabricators.

nakedness.

[12]Do not reveal your father's sister's nakedness; she is your father's kin.

[13]Do not reveal your mother's sister's nakedness; she is your mother's kin.

[14]Do not reveal your father's brother's nakedness: do not approach his wife; she is your aunt.

[15]Do not reveal your daughter-in-law's nakedness. She is your son's wife: Do not reveal her nakedness.

[16]Do not reveal your brother's wife's nakedness; she is your brother's nakedness.

---

daughter born of rape.

[12] The word **kin** and the word "flesh" are closely related in meaning.

[14] she is your aunt You are to consider her your aunt, although she is not a blood relative (compare "my uncle Ḥanam'el" [Jeremiah 32:12], although Ḥanam'el was not technically Jeremiah's uncle). ¶What will they do who derive their Commandments from the written Torah alone? Scripture does not explicitly prohibit sexual relations with the mother's brother's wife, nor with the paternal grandmother, nor with the maternal grandmother. Consequently, we need the Oral Tradition (possibly Scripture does not mention a mother's brother's wife because we can generalize from the case of the father's brother's wife, and also because it is alluded to in the *parasha* of *Qedoshim* [20:20]; the two other abovementioned relations are not mentioned, because Scripture deals only with behaviors that are known to occur).

[16] your brother's wife See also the passage, "When brothers

[17]Do not reveal the nakedness of a woman and her daughter. Do not take her son's daughter or her daughter's daughter to reveal her nakedness; they are kin: It is repulsiveness. [18]Do not take a woman unto her sister, to rival, to reveal her nakedness upon her, in her lifetime. [19]Do not approach a woman in her ritual impurity of separation to reveal her nakedness. [20]To your

---

live..." [Deuteronomy 25:5].

[17] Should you ask why relations with a daughter are nowhere explicitly prohibited, the answer is that such a prohibition is implied by the ban against sexual relations with **a woman and her daughter**. After you have slept with a woman, her daughter is forbidden to you, regardless of whether or not she is also *your* daughter [the *halakha* [Yevamot 97a] is that one's wife's daughter is forbidden, but not the daughter of a woman with whom one has had extramarital relations — Translator]. **kin** [Hebrew: *sha'ra*] Hebrew contains two synonyms: *sh'er* [:6] and *sha'ra.* The *'alef* in *sha'ra* would be vocalized with a schwa (like the *lamed* in "garment" [Hebrew: *salma*] [Exodus 22:8]) if it were not a guttural consonant. **[18] to rival** a fellow wife, in the sense of "her rival provoked her" [I Samuel 1:6]. The upcoming *parasha* of *Qedoshim* does not mention the punishment for having sexual relations with two sisters, just as it does not mention the punishment for sexual relations with a granddaughter. The commentator erred who said that Raḥel and Leah could not have been actual sisters, on the grounds that all human beings are alike forbidden to commit incest. You may ask, "How can GOD punish someone for committing crimes about which he was not warned?" — but he would answer that the descendants of Noaḥ *were* commanded not to engage in any of the incestuous practices listed here. His evidence is the phrase "all these abominations" [:27], which implies that non-Jews are held accountable for all of the abovementioned prohibitions. As others have already pointed out, however, this evidence is not conclusive. Scripture uses the phrase "all these abominations" in a general way, to denote *most* of these abominations — not literally *all* of them. You will come to know my own opinion on these matters in the *parasha* of *Vayyelekh* [*comment on* Deuteronomy 31:16]. **[19]** Sexual rela-

fellowman's wife do not give your cohabitation for seed, to be defiled through her. [21]Do not give of your seed to hand over to Molekh; do not desecrate the Name of your

---

tions with a menstruant are a more serious offense than incest. **[20]** Some people say that Scripture has already prohibited **your fellowman's wife** [Exodus 20:13]; but this specification is needed, to exclude a woman captured in war. The word **for seed** has been misinterpreted by people whose passions overpowered their reason. We can divide sexuality into three components:

1) procreation, without physical desire;
2) to restore health and physical equilibrium; and
3) sheer animal lust.

Scripture uses the word **for seed** to say that even if your intention is solely to raise progeny, relations with a married woman are still strictly forbidden (the subsequent verse, "Of your seed..." [:21], shows that "seed" means "progeny" in this context). Scripture goes on to say **to be defiled through her**, for whoever touches a married woman shall not become clean, but shall be forever defiled. **[21]** This verse does not apply to one's children through a non-Jewish woman (this is irrelevant to the case of a female war captive, if she converts to Judaism). **Molekh** the name of an idol. Our Sages, of blessed memory, have interpreted this word [Sanhedrin 64a] as a general term for anything that someone may set on a throne [Hebrew: *yamlikh*] to rule over him. In all likelihood, however, it is also the name of a specific Ammonite abomination [I Kings 11:7]. **to hand over** meaning, to burn — for this was the manner of its worship. Others say that the child was passed over a fire: some survived, and others died. Still others point out that the verse nowhere mentions fire, and that the commandment is not to hand a child over from the teachings of GOD into the worship of Molekh. By handing over the offspring of the holy nation to Molekh, you thereby desecrate **the Name** of your God, Who has called you into His service. ¶Sa'adya Gaon classified the sexual crimes into eight levels of vileness [*comment on* Exodus 20:13]. Worst of all is intercourse with a beast, because that involves an entirely different species. The next level of severity is intercourse with another man, because the entire gender is forbidden. A lower level of severity is intercourse with one's father's wife, and similar

God: I am GOD. [22]Do not lie with a male as one has coition with a woman: It is an abomination. [23]Do not give your ejaculation to any beast, to become defiled thereby. A woman may not stand before a beast to mount her: It is

---

relations who are always forbidden. I shall not belabor the point, because these classifications are not practically useful, insofar as all sexual offenses are punishable by *karet.* [22] **with a man** We have seen from the verse "I have lain with my father last night" [Genesis 19:34] that the verb "to lie" may be used both by men and by women to denote sexual intercourse. Thus, this commandment applies equally to a pederast and to a catamite. The phrase **coition with a woman** [literally: coitions with a woman] has caused a great deal of trouble, on account of the plural noun. Rabbi Ḥanan'el ben Ḥushi'el, may he rest in peace, said that there are men who graft something on to their bodies which has the appearance of the female organ. Others speak of a hermaphrodite. One person claims that Scripture here alludes to the two different ways one may have intercourse with a woman; therefore, homosexual intercourse is forbidden, whether it is done the standard way, or a nonstandard way. The truth is, in my opinion, that the commandment is to be understood simply and literally. The Hebrew word "coition" sometimes means "ejaculation"; this is why the word **coitions** appears in the plural. The Sages have declared that homosexual intercourse, like the other sexual crimes, is punishable by death [Yevamot 83b]. **Do not lie** Scripture speaks delicately, as in the phrase "Do not draw near" [:19]. Since Man was designed to be dominant, and Woman was designed to be submissive, Scripture warns us not to reverse the will of GOD. To dwell on this subject any further is distasteful. **It is an abomination** [Hebrew: *to'eva*] something which is naturally abhorred [Hebrew: *nit'av*] by a refined spirit. [23] **any beast** i.e., a female beast. I have already translated the word **your ejaculation** [Hebrew: *skhovtkha*] [*comment on* :22]; it is probably related to the word "lying down" [Hebrew: *skhiva*], because an emission typically occurs only after lying down. **to become defiled thereby** Scripture uses the same phrase concerning a married woman [:20] as it uses here concerning a beast. **before a beast** i.e., a male beast. **to mount her** the subject of this verb is the abovementioned beast: the woman is mounted upon, the object of

a destructive perversion. [24]Do not contaminate yourselves with any of these, for the nations I send away before you, were contaminated with all of these, [25]and the land was contaminated. I punished it for its sin, and the land vomited its inhabitants. [26]You shall observe my decrees and my judgments. Do not practice any of these abominations, neither the native nor the alien who dwells in your midst, [27]for the men of the land who preceded you practiced all these abominations, and the land became

---

the verb. The word is related to the Hebrew word for "four-legged". **It is a destructive perversion** The grammarians have classified this word as an 'ayin-'ayin word (like "the vanishing track of a snail" [Psalms 58:9]) with a superfluous *tav.* Thus it denotes destruction. Others assert that "flood" comes from the same root. It is related to the verb in "GOD confused the language of the whole Earth" [Genesis 11:9]. ¶In summary, Scripture mentions every category of creature that a man might encounter sexually, ranging from normal temptations like a married woman or a Gentile, all the way to a creature with which one cannot even have children (for an animal can mate successfully only with a member of its own species). **[24] Do not contaminate yourselves** The *ṭet* acquires a *dagesh* because it absorbs the *tav* of the *hitpa'el* (the fact that the *mem* has a *dagesh,* in accordance with the rule for a *hitpa'el* verb, indicates that the letter which the *ṭet* absorbed was *not* the *nun* of a *nif'al* verb). Scripture tells us that all of the abovementioned activities defile the soul. **I send away** they will either die, or be expelled **before you** not on your account, but on account of the holiness of the land. **[25] the land vomited** Whatever a man vomits is repugnant in his sight, and he does not return to it. **[26] observe My decrees** the abovementioned things which I have forbidden to you **and my judgments** you must render the justice that I demand, if anyone should disobey these laws. **Do not practice any of these abominations** Scripture repeats this admonition, in order to include **the alien**. These commandments apply equally to the native and to the resident alien, since both reside in the Holy Land. If you have sense in your head you shall understand that Ya'aqov (who in his day married two sisters in Ḥaran), and 'Amram after him (who

contaminated. [28]That the land not vomit you when you contaminate it — as it vomited the nation that preceded you. [29]For anyone who practices any of these abominations — the participating persons will be cut out from amid their people. [30]Observe My charge, to prevent yourselves from practicing any of the abominable customs which were practiced before you, so that you will not con-

---

married his aunt in Egypt), were not defiled by their actions. [27] **all these abominations** Both you and your descendants must realize this, so that you will keep the law, and the land will remain pure — otherwise, the land will vomit you out. **these** [Hebrew: *ha'el*] This word means the same as *ha'elleh* (compare, "those" [Hebrew: *hahem*] [Genesis 6:4] and "those" [Hebrew: *hahemma*] [Numbers 9:7]). However, Sa'adya Gaon disagrees. [28] **it vomited** either

- The verb is in the past tense, third person masculine singular, from the root q-'-h, as in "Drink, become drunk, and vomit" [Jeremiah 25:27] — the latter word also stems from q-'-h, as the four letters *'alef*, *heh*, *vav*, and *yod* often interchange with one another. We see elsewhere that the word "land" sometimes assumes the masculine gender, as in "the land is darkened" [Isaiah 9:18] and "the land was not able to support them" [Genesis 13:6].

or

- The verb is in the present tense, third person feminine singular, from the root q-v-', as in the similar *'ayin-vav* verb "approaching with the sheep" [Genesis 29:6] (normally, a shift into the present tense would be indicated by inserting a pronoun, so as to read "...as *she* is now vomiting out...").

[29] **the participating persons will be cut out** If they act in public, you shall execute them; if they act in private, I shall cut them off Myself. [30] **Observe My charge** This constitutes the charge: that you **prevent yourselves from practicing** etc. **which were practiced before you** A man must not say, "Since the ancients acted thus, I shall act this way also." **I am GOD your God** This relates to the previous phrase, **observe My charge**. A skeptic should not ask,

taminate yourselves with them: I am GOD, your God."

[19:1]GOD told Moshe: [2]Tell the entire community of the Children of Israel, and say to them: "Be holy, for I, GOD, your God, am holy. [3]Each of you will revere his mother and father. You will observe My Sabbaths; I am GOD,

---

"What is this charge for?" — for **I am GOD your God**; and you shall do all that I command you.

[19: 2] The entire community of the Children of Israel means that the resident alien is not included. Like the Israelites, resident aliens were told not to commit any sexual offenses; therefore they must now be specifically excluded from most of the subsequent commandments. However, Scripture mentions the current passage immediately after the passage dealing with sexual offenses, so that one should not think that resident aliens may remain in the land, if they refrain *only* from sexual crimes. In fact, there are other commandments which they must follow in order not to be expelled from the land: i.e., the Ten Commandments which are herein mentioned. ¶**Be holy** This is the prohibition against idolatry. It is given on account of the fact that **I, GOD your God, am holy** (which corresponds to the utterance that most people count as the First Commandment). "Do not swear by My name..." [:12] corresponds to the Commandment "You shall not swear..." [Exodus 20:7]. **[3] You will observe My Sabbaths** corresponds to "Remember the Sabbath day..." [Exodus 20:8]; **Each of you will revere his mother and father** corresponds to "Honor your father and your mother..." [Exodus 20:12]; and "Do not stand idle when your fellowman is in danger" [:16] corresponds to the Commandment "You shall not murder" [Exodus 20:13]. The passage of the betrothed bondmaid [:20] warns us not to commit adultery with a freewoman. "Do not steal; do not deny; do not lie" [:11] and "Do not exploit your neighbor" [:13] correspond to the three remaining Commandments. I have already told you in the *parasha* of *Mishpaṭim* [*comment on* Exodus 21:2] that every commandment is self-contained, but that nevertheless, there are associations among the commandments that account for their juxtaposition in the verses. The *parasha* of *Qedoshim* begins with the commandment,

your God. [4]Do not turn to the idols; do not make gods of molten images for yourselves; I am GOD, your God. [5]If you sacrifice a peace-offering to GOD, offer it of your own free will. [6]On the day you slaughter it it may be eaten,

---

each of you will revere [*plural*] **his mother and father**. Scripture has already said [Exodus 20:12] that whoever *honors* his parents will enjoy long life; consequently, whoever *dishonors* his parents shortens his life, and Scripture accordingly tells us to fear our parents as well as to honor them. The verse mentions the mother before mentioning the father, because a child at first recognizes only his mother. Later, he recognizes his father. Afterwards he recognizes the Sabbath (it is incumbent upon a child to observe the Sabbath, unlike the remaining festivals). Eventually he will come to recognize his God, Who rested on the seventh day. The next logical obligation is "Do not turn to the idols" [:4]. We know from tradition what constitutes "reverence" of one's parents. Scripture employs brevity by using only one instance of the word *'ish* to signify **Each of you** [Hebrew: *'ish 'ish*]. The plural form of the verb **revere** informs us that anyone who sees the law being broken must teach and compel the lawbreaker to change. The same principle applies to keeping the Sabbath, since the plural form **you shall observe** is used. **I am GOD your God** You shall do as I do, Who rested from all labor. **[4] Do not turn** Do not even direct your attention to them by looking at them. **idols** [Hebrew: *'elilim*] i.e., graven images. They are called *'elilim* because they are false, as in "you are all physicians of no value [Hebrew: *'elil*]" [Job 13:4]. It is also plausible that the word comes from *'el*, meaning something that lacks substance. **molten images** which supposedly receive their power from the heavens. There is no need for any God other than Me; therefore Scripture states, **I am GOD your God**. The verb **turn** is in plural form, as is the verb **make**, to teach us that whoever sees such a thing, and does not reveal it, is considered an accomplice. **[5] If you sacrifice a peace-offering** This is connected to the previous verse: They shall not offer sacrifices to the demons, who are false gods, but rather shall offer sacrifices only to GOD. The verb **sacrifice** is in plural form, because Scripture speaks of the most common case, when several people join together to offer a single sacrifice. **of your own free will** They should bring the sacrifice wil-

and on the next day; what remains until the third day will be burned in fire. [7]If it is eaten on the third day it is offensive; it will not be accepted. [8]Whoever eats it will suffer his iniquity, for he has desecrated what GOD has sanctified: That person will be cut off from his people. [9]When you reap the harvest of your land: Do not finish off the corner of your field in reaping; do not gather the individual stalks of your harvest; [10]do not glean your vineyard; do not gather the fallen grapes of your vine-yard. Leave them for the poor and for the alien: I am

---

lingly, and not out of compulsion. **[8] Whoever eats** [*plural*] **will suffer** [*singular*] Each one of the people who eat it, as in "The righteous [*plural*] are secure [*singular*] like a lion" [Proverbs 28:1] [*cf. comment on* Deuteronomy 7:10]. **he has desecrated what GOD has sanctified** Once he has offered the sacrifice to the Most High, all of its flesh is holy. The word **desecrated** [Hebrew: *ḥillel*] is related to "secular" [Hebrew: *ḥol*]. This verse specifies the punishment for a commandment which has already appeared [7:18] — namely, **that person will be cut off. [9]** The reason for mentioning **When you reap...** after mentioning the peace-offering, is that we must allocate our harvest the same way we allocate the sacrificial portions of a peace-offering: for the glory of GOD, for the poor, and for the alien. The word **When you reap** is grammatically bizarre, because it is a verbal noun derived from the *qal* form [and the *qof* should be vocalized with a *qamaṣ qaṭan*]. **the corner of your field** One must leave *one* corner of the field unharvested. **individual stalks** This word has a precise meaning [Pe'a 6:5]. **[10] do not glean** [Hebrew: *t'olel*] **your vineyard** Do not obliterate the *'olelot*, the young, immature grapes (from the word "child" [Hebrew: *'olel*] [Jeremiah 44:7]), sometimes called the "sucklings". This is a denominalized verb, as in "root you out of the land of the living" [Psalms 52:7] (meaning, he will destroy the roots), and "branches the bough" [Isaiah 10:33] (meaning, he will destroy the branch).[1] **fallen grapes** This term is known from tradition [Pe'a 7:3]. It is related to "pluck the strings of the lute" [Amos 6:5]. **for the poor** of Israel **and for**

---

[1] [*cf.* English "to weed", "to peel" — Translator]

GOD, your God. [11]Do not steal; do not deny; and do not lie to one another. [12]Do not swear by My Name falsely, that you desecrate the Name of your God: I am GOD. [13]Do not exploit your neighbor. Do not rob. The hire of a laborer shall not remain the night with you until morning. [14]Do not curse the deaf. Before the blind do not place a stumbling block. Revere your God: I am GOD. [15]Do not pervert justice: Do not elevate the face of a poor man, and do not glorify the face of a great man. In

---

the alien "who dwell among you" – i.e., the converts. **[11] Do not steal** follows the previous verse, in order to say: Since I have commanded you, for the glory of GOD, to give your own possessions to the poor, certainly you must not take someone else's possessions! The plural form of the verb **Do not steal** teaches us that whoever witnesses a theft, and remains silent, is also considered a thief. **Do not deny** [*plural*] regarding a deposit entrusted to you; and whoever knows the truth but does not testify is also guilty of denial. **do not lie** by demanding money from someone who does not owe you anything. **[12] Do not swear by My Name falsely** appears after "Do not steal...", for someone who is accused of stealing, or of denying a deposit, must take an oath. Scripture uses the plural form of the verb, to include as well anyone who induces another to swear falsely. **desecrate** Whoever swears falsely denies GOD, as I have explained [*comment on* Exodus 20:7]. **[13] Do not exploit your neighbor** covertly **and do not rob** overtly, by force of arms **hire** i.e., wages, as in "his hire is before him" [Isaiah 40:10]. Most likely the word's origin is elliptical, from "(the reward of someone's) hire". Many people apply this verse to the case of a day laborer. One must not say, "Come and do the same work tomorrow **morning**, and in the morning I shall give you two days' wages." The Exegetes have demonstrated [Bava Meṣi'a 110b] that this verse discusses a day laborer, because elsewhere Scripture says, "before the sun sets" [Deuteronomy 24:15] concerning a night laborer. **[14] Do not curse** [even] **the deaf**, although you may have the power to do so with impunity. Similarly, do not place a stumbling block **before the blind**. **Revere your God** Who can punish you, although your victims cannot, and can strike you deaf or blind.

righteousness shall you judge your fellowman. [16]Do not go as a talebearer among your people. Do not stand idle when your fellowman is in danger: I am GOD. [17]Do not hate your brother in your heart; reprove your fellowman; and do not bear sin because of him. [18]Do not take vengeance, and do not bear a grudge against the Children of your People. Love to your fellowman as yourself: I am

---

[15] **Do not pervert justice** This commandment is directed to judges and witnesses. **a great man** here denotes a wealthy man (*cf.* the description of Barzillai [II Samuel 19:33]). [16] **a talebearer** from the word "your merchandise" [Ezekiel 28:16] and also "...with all powders of the merchant" [Song of Songs 3:6]. Here the word denotes a gossiper. Just as a merchant transmits things, buying them here and selling them there, so also does a gossiper transmit things, revealing to one what he heard from another. **Do not stand idle when your fellowman is in danger** [literally: Do not stand upon your fellowman's blood] One must not become involved with men who shed blood. It is well known that many people have been murdered, many people have been killed, because of slander. Doeg the Edomite is a prime example [I Samuel 22:9–19]. **I am GOD** Who sees all that you do in private. [17] **Do not hate your brother** This is the negative aspect of "love your fellowman as yourself" [:18]. Although these commandments all involve a person's private emotions, only through their observance will Israel be permitted to remain on its land (The Second Temple was destroyed because of groundless hatred [Yoma 9b]). Perhaps you hate someone because you suspect him of something which never happened; therefore, **reprove your fellowman**. On the other hand, perhaps he actually did something which calls for reproof. In that case, **do not bear sin because of him**; because if you do not correct him, you might be punished on his account. [18] **Do not take vengeance, and do not bear a grudge** These terms are defined in the writings of our Sages [e.g., Yoma 23a]. **love to your fellowman as yourself** Many people have said that the *lamed* is superfluous, like the *lamed* in "they killed 'Avner" [II Samuel 3:30] [literally: they killed *to* 'Avner]. In my opinion, however, it contributes to the verse's meaning. One must love the good that pertains *to* one's fellowman as much as one

GOD. [19]Observe My decrees: Do not interbreed different kinds of animals; do not sow your field with something intermingled. An intermingled garment, wool and linen, shall not go up upon you. [20]If a man lies with a woman in coition, and she is a bondmaid subservient to a man, but she was not redeemed, nor was her freedom given to her – there will be lashes. They will not die, because she

---

loves the good that pertains *to* oneself. **I am GOD** means: I, a single God, have created all of you. **[19]** The reason for mentioning **Do not interbreed different kinds of animals** after the previous commandments, is to say to us: Just as the requirement to be holy implies that you must not do violence to other human beings, so also it implies that you must not do anything to animals which alters the work of GOD. This is why Scripture says, **Preserve My decrees**: you must *preserve* each species, and not interbreed one species with another. **intermingled** composed of two species. Later, I shall explain this word more fully. Not to intermingle even a field or a garment serves as a reminder. There are many commandments that are primarily reminders: e.g., the Festivals of Maṣṣot [Deuteronomy 16:3] and of Sukkot [23:43]; wearing *ṣiṣit* [Numbers 15:40]; hearing the *shofar* [Numbers 10:10]; affixing a *mzuza*; and wearing *tfillin* [Exodus 13:9]. I shall now reveal a little-known principle: Whoever is complete in his intellectual understanding is necessarily also complete in his religious observance. Thus, Scripture says regarding Abraham that "he kept My observances, My moral decrees, My authoritative decrees, and My laws" [Genesis 26:5]. **wool and linen** mixed together. This word is unique in Scripture. The Exegetes have said [Kil'ayyim 9:8] that it is a compound word, formed from three smaller words. It may also stem from a five-letter root. **[20] a bondmaid** The Exegetes have asserted that this woman is not Jewish. Otherwise, a literal interpretation of this verse would identify her with the Israelite woman who is discussed in the passage "When a man sells his daughter to be a maid-servant..." [Exodus 21:7]. In both cases, the woman has been designated eventually to marry her master, or her master's son, but she is not formally engaged. This is the meaning of **she was not free** – for she does not become completely free un-

was not free. [21]He will bring his guilt-offering to GOD at the entrance of the Tent of Assembly: a ram guilt-

---

til she receives a proper betrothal. **subservient** [Hebrew: *neḥerefet*] Most people render this word as "designated to"; but in my opinion, the word comes from "shame" [Hebrew: *ḥerpa*]. She is ashamed because she is a bondmaid, and because she is an unbetrothed virgin living in someone else's household. **redeemed** a verbal noun from the passive, *hof'al* form. Neither her father nor any other relative redeemed her before she became of age. **her freedom** The word is vocalized with a *shuruq*. Normally, a *qamaṣ qaṭan* would be expected, because the base noun is pronounced *ḥofesh*, vocalized with a *ḥolem*. It was conventional to write the girl a bill of manumission [and to marry her – Translator] before a fixed amount of time had elapsed, if her father sold her into slavery [Bekhorot 13a]. The Exegetes said [Karetot 11a; Giṭṭin 43b] that the verse discusses a woman who is half free and half slave; and their words are true. **lashes** [Hebrew: *biqqoret*] Some people interpret the word to mean "concubine", claiming that the word is related to "king's daughters were among your honorable ones" [Hebrew: *biqqrotekha*] [Psalms 45:10]. This interpretation is incorrect, as *biqqrotekha* denotes "the *valuable* maidservants". The *yod* of the triliteral root y-q-r disappears, because the preposition which precedes it is vocalized with a *ḥiriq* (otherwise, the word would contain two adjacent voiced schwas – one underneath the preposition, and one underneath the first root-letter – and the Hebrew language does not tolerate such a combination). This rule is obeyed everywhere.[1] Others say that *biqqoret* comes from "the kohen will not seek" [Hebrew: *yevaqqer*] [13:36], meaning, to search for something. The Exegetes have said that she is flogged with a strap made of cowhide [Hebrew: *baqar*]. Although this is true on the basis of tradition, the etymology is only a mnemonic. The reason this commandment is mentioned in the current passage is that whoever disobeys it cheats the bondmaid's owner. That is why **[21]** he must bring a ram guilt-offering. Another, more figurative, explanation is that this act of sexual intercourse is also a kind of intermixture – a

---

[1]with one exception: "Many of them that sleep [Hebrew: *miyysheney*] in the dust of the earth shall awake" [Daniel 12:2], following the text of Moses Ben-Naftali.

offering. [22]The kohen will secure atonement for him with the ram guilt-offering before GOD for the sin he committed. he will be forgiven for the sin he committed.

[23]When you come to the land and plant any kind of food tree, you must leave its fruit unused: For three years it will be forbidden to you. It shall not be eaten. [24]In the fourth year, all its fruit will be holiness of praisegiving to GOD. [25]In the fifth year, you may eat of its fruit. To in-

---

mixing of freeman and slavewoman. **[22] he will be forgiven** I will explain this later at greater length [*comment on* Numbers 14:19].

[23] Having mentioned the sowing of crops [:19], and the sowing of a woman [:20] (who is analogous to the soil), Scripture proceeds to things that are planted, and discusses the forbidden fruits. It is well known that fruit which grows on trees less than three years old is harmful and contains no nutrition (just as fish that do not have fins and scales are harmful, and meat from birds of prey and from the non-kosher beasts is detrimental to the intelligence — *verbum sat sapienti*). **you will leave its fruit unused** [literally: you shall regard the fruit as uncircumcised] You shall treat it as you treat a foreskin, which is harmful and serves no purpose (linguistically, a foreskin [Hebrew: *'orla*] is an "impediment" of the flesh, like a speech impediment [Hebrew: *'orla*], or a hearing impediment [Hebrew: *'orla*]). **unused** Literally means to treat something as an *'orla*; but the Aramaic translation is also worthy of note ["You shall put it aside for destruction"]. **it will be forbidden** as a consequence of having regarded it as uncircumcised. **[24] praisegiving** In order to praise GOD. This fruit must be eaten by the kohanim. **[25] increase its produce** This is a continuation of the previous verse: The fruit is designated for praisegiving, because He shall **increase its produce**. Although the two parts of the sentence are far removed from one another, there are other places in Scripture also where intervening phrases break the syntax of a connected idea. To pick one example out of many: "He must make restitution; if he has nothing wherewith to pay..." [Exodus 22:2] is a displaced continuation of the verse "he shall pay five oxen for every

crease its produce for you. I am GOD, your God. [26]Do not eat on blood. Do not believe in omens. Do not believe in auspicious times. [27]Do not cut off the hair on the corners

---

ox..." [Exodus 21:37]. **I am GOD** i.e., I am capable of increasing My blessing over your crops. **[26] Do not eat on blood** This commandment (which prohibits eating meat from any of the permitted species of animals until its blood is dashed upon the Altar of GOD) logically follows the previous one (which prohibits eating fruit from a domesticated tree until the fifth year). It applies only in the vicinity of the Sanctuary, and this is borne out by Sha'ul's words [I Samuel 14:34], for he had the Ark with him [I Samuel 14:18]. By saying [I Samuel 14:33] that they were "eating on blood", it is as if Scripture accused them of eating sacrifices to the satyrs. As I have explained, it was an Egyptian custom to offer sacrifices to demons; and if one has not dashed the blood against the Altar in the name of GOD, it is apparent that one is eating in the name of demons. For this reason the commandment is juxtaposed to **Do not believe in omens**: The Egyptians used to eat on blood, and stray after the demons; the Canaanites used to believe in omens, and in propitious times (as it is written [Deuteronomy 18:14]). Once again Scripture associates Egyptian and Canaanite practices, as expressed earlier by "the deeds of the land of Egypt...the deeds of the land of Canaan" [18:3]. People look for omens to test things about which they are uncertain, as in "I have tested you by divination, and have established that GOD has blessed me..." [Genesis 30:27]. Shapes, special rods, unusual events, and arbitrary movements have all been used as omens, as well as days of the year or hours of the day. **Do not believe in auspicious times** [Hebrew: *lo t'onenu*] Some people say that this word comes from "answer" [Hebrew: *'ana*]: one concentrates on some particular question, and listens carefully to something to hear how he will be answered. This etymology is grammatically unacceptable. Other people relate the word to "her scheduled times" [Hebrew: *'onatah*] [Exodus 21:10]. In my opinion the word derives from "cloud" [Hebrew: *'anan*]. It is well known that people perform divination on clouds, by observing their shapes and their movements. The word is most likely an *'ayin-'ayin* verb (as in "to turn" [Hebrew: s-b-b]). Here the verb is in the *polel* form. It appears in the *qal* form in "soothsayers like the Philistines" [Isaiah 2:6]. A clearer example is found in "a diviner of auspicious times,

of your head. Do not destroy the corners of your beard.
[28]Do not make any incision in your flesh for the soul. Do
not put tattoo marks within you; I am GOD. [29]Do not
desecrate your daughter by prostituting her. You will then not make the land sexually immoral, and the land full of repulsiveness. [30]Observe My Sabbaths, and revere

---

or a diviner of omens" [Deuteronomy 18:10]. [27] At this point Scripture mentions **Do not cut off the hair on the corners of your head** because this too was the practice of the other nations; and we must separate ourselves from them. Moreover, the hair on the head and the beard were created for beauty, and it is inappropriate to destroy it. Some people suggest that this verse precedes [28] **Do not make any incision in your flesh** because it was a sign of mourning to cut off the hair on the corners of the head, or on the corners of the beard. **incision** The meaning of this word, like that of the abovementioned "corners" of the head and of the beard, is known to us through tradition [Makkot 20b]. **for the soul** here denotes a dead body (as it is correctly rendered in the Aramaic translation). The *nun* is not doubled with a *dagesh* for the sake of ease of pronunciation. **tattoo marks** Some say that this commandment is connected to the previously-mentioned **incision** because there are people who tattoo themselves as a sign of mourning, using fire to brand their body with specific shapes. Nowadays, also, people mark their faces when they are young in order to distinguish themselves. The word **tattoo** is doubled, like "and that which comes out of it" [Isaiah 42:5]. It comes from "and have them impale" [Numbers 25:4]. The opinion of the Aramaic translator, however, seems to be that the word has no cognate, and this too is plausible. [29] After discussing gashes in the skin for the dead, Scripture now mentions **Do not desecrate your daughter**, because she must not be uncovered in public. Even a woman's voice is indecent [Berakhot 24a] — how much more so, incisions in her flesh. **You will then not make the land sexually immoral** Scripture employs metonymy, and means sexual immorality among the *inhabitants* of the land. Compare, "when the land sins against me" [Ezekiel 14:12]. [30] The injunction to **observe My Sabbaths** appears next, after mentioning the dead — to remind us that there is no mourning on the Sabbath. However, the principle of **revere My**

My Sanctuary: I am GOD. [31]Do not turn to charmers or wizards; do not seek out, to be defiled by them: I am GOD, your God. [32]Stand up for the elderly, honor the face of the aged, and revere your God: I am GOD.

[33]If a convert dwells with you in your land, do not mis-

---

sanctuary applies to the High Priest, who must not behave like other mourners (this warning extends to all people associated with the Sanctuary). **I am GOD** that is to say, those who do not revere My Sanctuary, and honor it, shall be punished. [31] Having brought up the dead, Scripture now mentions **charmers and wizards**, since they purport to communicate with the dead (as it is written in Isaiah, "[seek guidance] of the dead on behalf of the living" [Isaiah 8:19]). **charmers** [Hebrew: *'ovot*] as in "jugs" [Hebrew: *'ovot*] [Job 32:19] – this being a major tool of their trade. **wizards** [Hebrew: *yidd'onim*], from "knowledge" [Hebrew: *da'at*]. They seek knowledge of the future. Certain empty-headed people have asserted that Scripture would not have forbidden charmers as a form of witchcraft if they were not true. I declare the exact opposite of their words: Scripture has forbidden only that which is false, but has not forbidden the truth. This is borne out by the prohibitions against idols and graven images. Were it not for my unwillingness to enter into a digression, I could elucidate definitive proofs against this practice. **Do not turn** to learn the art. **Do not seek** to request their services (as Saul did [I Samuel 28:8]). **I am GOD your God** You must seek out GOD alone. That is why Scripture uses the phrase **defiled by them**: anyone who turns to or who seeks out these forms of magic defiles his soul, because he detaches himself from GOD. [32] After discussing the dead, Scripture says **Stand up for the elderly**, for an aged man is close to death, and his body is already considered dead. This commandment includes every old person and every person with white hair [Qiddushin 32b]. **Revere your God** Who can punish you in your old age.

[33] **If a convert dwells with you** is mentioned after the elderly. Just as Scripture has admonished you to honor an elderly Israelite though he has no power, so does it admonish you regarding a convert, who also has little power compared to you (perhaps he is

treat him. [34]The convert who lives with you will be to
you like a resident among you. You will love to him like
yourself; for you were strangers in the land of Egypt: I
am GOD, your God. [35]Do not act dishonestly in judging:
whether in length, in weight, or in volume. [36] You will
have just scales, just stones, a just *'efa*, and a just *hin*. I
am GOD, your God, Who took you out of the land of
Egypt. [37]Observe all My decrees and all My rational precepts, and practice them: I am GOD."

[20:1]GOD told Moshe: [2]Tell the Children of Israel: Any
man of the Children of Israel, or of the alien that dwells
with Israel, who gives any of his children to Molech, will

---

considered powerless simply because he resides in your land, under your dominion). **[34] you will love to him** already explained [*comment on* :18]. **[35] Do not act dishonestly** mentioned here on account of the convert — as in, "execute justice between a man and his neighbor, and even a convert" [Deuteronomy 1:16]. Similarly, do not act deceitfully when you measure length. This clearly implies, since the units of length differ from place to place, that you must deal in terms that are commonly used in your location. **[36] just scales, just stones** an elaboration on measures of weight **a just *'efa*** a unit of dry measure **a just *hin*** a unit of liquid measure — these are both measures of volume. **I am GOD, your God, Who took you out ...** I have already reminded you that "you were strangers in the land of Egypt" [:34]; and consequently, **[37]** you must keep **My decrees** and **My rational precepts** in your hearts, and you must obey them in practice. **I am GOD** i.e., you must pursue the fulfillment of the precepts which I have given you, for they are entirely just.

[20:1] GOD told Moshe The preceding commandments are binding upon Israel, to the exclusion of the resident alien (which is why they were introduced by "Tell the entire community of the [Children of] Israel" [19:2]). Scripture is now about to describe punishments for sexual crimes, which are applicable to anyone who

die. The people of the land will stone him with a stone. [3]I will turn My anger against that man and will cut him out from amid his people; for he has given of his seed to Molech for the sake of defiling My Sanctuary and desecrating My holy Name. [4]If the People of Israel avert their eyes from that man as he gives of his seed to Molech, in order not to kill him, [5]I Myself will turn My anger against that man, and against his family. I will cut him off — and all who are deluded with him, to stray after the Molekh — from amid their people. [6]The person who turns to charmers and wizards, to stray after them — I will turn My anger against that person, and I will cut

---

lives in the land of Israel — native and alien alike. **[2] who gives any of his children to Molekh** This is the gravest of all sexual crimes: to sleep with an idolater, and to father her children. Thus it is mentioned first. **The people of the land** The land where he dwells, whether as a native or as a foreigner. This punishment is imposed only if the crime was perpetrated in public. **with a stone** We might think that this is a collective noun, as in "I have ox and donkey" [Genesis 32:6]; however, the words of the tradition [Sanhedrin 45a] are true. **[3] I will turn My anger against that man** if the crime was committed in secret. Some people say that this denotes destruction of his progeny. **defiling My Sanctuary** which resides in the land of Israel. **desecrating My holy Name** for the other nations will hear of it. **[5]** Rabbi Yona ibn Janakh has said that **his family** refers to the case when his family follows him into crime. What is the rabbi's problem? Clearly the plain and straightforward explanation is preferable: the inhabitants of the land might ignore his crime, because they are members of his family. **and all who are deluded with him** If he does not die, he will lead others astray. **[6] the person who turns to charmers** Just as I shall destroy whoever gives his children to Molekh secretly — or who does it in public, if the inhabitants of the land do not execute him — so shall I destroy whoever strays away from Me and turns to **charmers and wizards**. The Hebrew word *nefesh* appears in the masculine plural in the phrase "the people that you hunt" [Ezekiel

**him out from amid his people. [7]Sanctify yourselves, and
be holy, for I am GOD, your God. [8]Observe My statutes
and practice them: I am GOD, Who consecrates you.
[9]Any man who curses his father and his mother will die:
he cursed his father or his mother; he alone is to blame
for his death. [10]If a man commits adultery with a married woman: he has committed adultery with his**

13:20]; it is masculine singular in "fourteen people in all" [Genesis 46:22]. Similarly, here it is the masculine antecedent of the phrase **I will cut him off.** **[7] Sanctify yourselves...for I am GOD, your God** Who am holy; **[8]** and I have given you decrees for you to keep, in order to make you holy. This idea was expressed earlier [11:44] and it is repeated here to include the foreigners who live among Israel. They must keep themselves holy, because they live in the Holy Land. **[9]** Scripture now mentions the punishments for the crimes that were listed at the beginning of the *parasha*, starting with "Each of you will be in awe of his mother and father" [19:3]. Here the father is mentioned first, out of respect. **Any man who curses his father and his mother** Scripture employs ellipsis, and means "Any man who curses his father, and any man who curses his mother". **he cursed his father or his mother** That is to say: He has done a horrible thing. **he alone is to blame for his death** [literally: his blood is with him] compare, "his blood is on his head" [Joshua 2:19]. The tradition which we have received from our ancestors, and upon which we rely, sees in this phrase an allusion to the form of execution which does not cause external bleeding — i.e., stoning.[1] Without the tradition, we would not know how to go about executing someone. We would also not know how old a person must be to be responsible for his crimes, since Scripture does not say so explicitly. **[10]** The punishment for **If a man commits adultery with a married woman** is now mentioned (the prohibition has already been given [18:20]). **He has committed adultery with his neighbor's wife** The same device is used in the previous verse ("He cursed his father or his mother" [:9]) and in both cases the repetition means: He has done a horrible thing. ¶The woman

---

[1]Actually, neither stoning nor strangulation causes external bleeding.

neighbor's wife; the adulterer and the adulteress must die. [11]A man who lies with his father's wife: he has uncovered his father's nakedness; they must both die; their blood is with them. [12]A man who lies with his daughter-in-law: they must both die; they have practiced a destructive perversion; their blood is with them. [13]A man who lies with a male as one has coition with a woman: both have committed an abomination; they must die; their blood is with them. [14]If a man marries a woman and her mother — it is lewdness. They will burn him and them; there will be no lewdness among you. [15]A man who gives his ejaculation within a beast shall die. You shall kill the beast. [16]A woman who approaches any beast to perform bestiality with her — you must kill the woman, and the animal will die. Their blood is with them. [17]If a man marries his sister, his father's daughter or his mother's daughter; and he saw her nakedness, and she sees his nakedness — it is a shameful perversion. They will be cut off in the sight of the Children of their People. He un-

---

is not called an **adulteress** if she was raped. **[11] he has uncovered his father's nakedness** i.e., he has committed a serious crime. **[12] daughter-in-law** This term denotes a son's wife. **a destructive perversion** I have already explained this word [*comment on* 18:23]. **[13] they have committed** [*plural*] **an abomination** The plural form of the verb applies only if the catamite was not raped. **[14] If a man marries a woman ... it is lewdness** i.e., an incestuous act was contemplated. **and them** i.e., either one or the other. If the mother was his original wife, the daughter will be burnt, and *vice versa*. **[15] you shall kill the animal** so that it not cause another person to sin. There are also some who say: in order to conceal the disgrace. **[16] to perform bestiality** This word is an infinitive, even though the first letter of the triliteral root is vocalized with a *ḥiriq* (compare, "When I break off" [26:26]). Verbal nouns in Hebrew assume various forms. **[17] If a man marries his sister** Such a

covered his sister's nakedness: he will bear his sin. [18] If a man has coition with an indisposed woman, if he revealed her nakedness, he has violated her womb. She has revealed her the source of her blood, and they shall both will be cut out from amid their people. [19] The nakedness of your mother's sister and of your father's sister you shall not reveal. He has violated his near kin. They shall bear

---

marriage must have been performed by people unaware of their relationship, which subsequently became known. **and he saw her nakedness** that is, "*or* he sees ..." (as in, "he cursed his father, or his mother" [:9]). In this context, the word **saw** is synonymous with "uncovered". **and she sees his nakedness** thus the act occurred by mutual consent. **a shameful perversion** [Hebrew: *ḥesed*] from "lest the hearer put you to shame" [Proverbs 25:10]. The word denotes an egregious sexual crime. **He uncovered his sister's nakedness** If he forced her, then **he** alone **will bear his sin**. ¶Scripture chooses to make the above points in the case of a brother and a sister because they grow up together, they play together when young, and frequently they are left alone together. Conversely, Scripture does not mention the punishment for sleeping with one's son's daughter or one's daughter's daughter, relegating it instead to the Oral Law, because a man is normally advanced in years and empty of desire by the time he has a mature granddaughter. For the same reason, Scripture does not mention the case of a father's mother or a mother's mother — because they are old. **[18] indisposed** She is considered ill, because she loses blood. **he has violated her womb** that is, he has committed an abominable act. **she has revealed** voluntarily; but if she is forced, he alone will be cut off. **[19]** If you uncover **your mother's sister's nakedness**, which I have already told you not to uncover [18:13], you fall into the category one who has **violated his near kin**. If it was done deliberately, **they shall bear their guilt**. However, Scripture does not state the punishment for intercourse with one's aunt. Similarly, Scripture does not even mention that there *is* a punishment for intercourse with two sisters. A learned person will understand why [out of respect for 'Amram, who married his aunt, and for Ya'aqov, who married two sisters — Translator] [*cf. comment on*

their guilt. [20]Someone who lies with his aunt has revealed his uncle's nakedness. They will carry their sin: They will die childless. [21]Someone who takes his brother's wife — she is separated. He has revealed his brother's nakedness; they will die childless. [22]You will observe all My decrees, and all My precepts, and you will practice them; that the land to which I bring you to dwell

---

18:26]. The words of the tradition are also true [Yevamot 3b]. **[20] his aunt** In Hebrew, this word only denotes the wife of one's uncle. **childless** [Hebrew: *'aririm*] The Sadducees [a derogatory reference to Karaites — Translator] claim that this word is a synonym for "naked" [Hebrew: *'arumim*] [Genesis 2:25] and that **they will die** means "they will be executed"; but they are wrong. The Aramaic translation is correct. I have elsewhere explained the phrase "write this man childless" [Jeremiah 22:30] along the lines of "I remain childless" [Genesis 15:2]. **[21]** A brother's wife is said to be **separated**, i.e., it is proper to distance oneself from her (compare, "your brethren that hated you, that cast you out" [Isaiah 66:5]). Of all the prohibited sexual relations, this word is used only in connection with a brother's wife. Just as a woman enters her monthly period of separation, during which she is forbidden, and after which in time she becomes permitted, so also can a brother's wife become permitted (see my comment on the passage "When brothers live together ..." [Deuteronomy 25:5]). ¶Certain people have said that just as it is forbidden for a man to have relations with his father's sister, so it must be forbidden for a woman to marry her uncle. This reasoning is not valid. The prohibited relations are all specified from the man's point of view, because it is possible for a man to force sexual relations with someone else, whereas it is not possible for a woman to force sexual relations on a man. According to their line of reasoning, let them explain why we do not accept the testimony of two women! Even if one follows the standard valuations [27:2], four female witnesses should be at least as good as two male witnesses. Accordingly, we require the tradition. **[22] You will observe all My decrees** by abstaining from these incestuous relations. **and all My precepts** by carrying out the specified punishments. **so that the land will not vomit** I shall explain this in

therein, will not vomit you. [23]Do not follow the customs of the nation I am dispersing before you, for they did all of these, and I abhorred them. [24]I have said to you: You will inherit their land. I will give it to you to inherit — a land flowing milk and honey. I am GOD, your God; I have distinguished you from the nations. [25]You will distinguish between the ritually pure and the ritually impure beast, and between the ritually impure and the ritually pure bird. Do not make yourselves detestable through the beast, or the bird, or anything that creeps on the ground that I have set apart for you to consider ritually impure. [26]You will be holy to Me, for I, GOD, am holy; I have distinguished you from the nations, to be Mine. [27] A man or a woman in whom there is charming or wizardry — they shall die; They will stone them with stone; their blood is

---

the *parasha* of *Vayyelekh* [*comment on* Deuteronomy 31:16]. **[23] I abhorred them** An anthropomorphism, as in "His soul was disgusted" [Judges 10:16]. **[24] a land flowing milk and honey** There will be no land to resemble it. Just as **I have distinguished you from the nations** through these statutes, **[25]** So must you distinguish among the animals. **the ritually pure beast** The ten enumerated animals [Deuteronomy 14:4] are kosher; all the others are unkosher. **the ritually impure bird** Any bird mentioned [11:13] is unkosher; all the others are kosher. **to consider ritually impure** i.e., you must know, in thought and in speech, that they are ritually impure. Compare, "you shall consider detestable among the birds" [11:13]. For this reason a resident alien may not eat an unkosher species of animal in the Holy Land — and it is only on this condition that he may live among us. **[26]** If you observe everything I have commanded you, then you will become **holy**; for you are obliged to follow Me, and **I am holy**. **[27]** Previously, when charmers were mentioned, Scripture used the phrase "to be defiled by them" [19:31]. Now that Scripture tells us that we must be holy, we are told to execute anyone who defiles his soul through charming or through wizardry (up until now, the punishment for performing these prac-

in them.

[21:1]GOD told Moshe: Speak to the kohanim, the children of Aaron, and say to them: He will not defile himself with a soul among his people, [2]except for his nearest kin — for his mother, for his father, for his son, for his daughter, and for his brother. [3]And for his virgin sister who is near to him, who has not been with a man — for her he may

---

tices in public was not specified). The case of a woman is singled out, because women are more involved in these professions than men are (compare, "You shall not spare a witch" [Exodus 22:17]).

[21:1] Speak to the kohanim After commanding the Children of Israel (including the children of Aaron) to be holy [19:2], Scripture now commands **the children of Aaron** to observe additional restrictions, because they are dedicated to GOD 's service. It is also possible that **Speak to the kohanim** means: Teach the kohanim the previous *parasha* — because the propagation of the Torah has been entrusted to them — whereas **and say to them** refers to the upcoming commandments, which they alone must follow. **with a soul** this means, with a dead person. **defile himself** This verb is in the *hitpa'el* form. Its *ṭet* acquires a *dagesh* because it absorbs the preceding *tav*. **among his people** among all Israel, which is his nation. **[2] except for his nearest kin** We might think that this is a general category, which is then followed by particulars (e.g., **for his mother, for his father,** etc.), as in the phrase "No one shall come close to his near kin" [18:6]. Furthermore, we might think that the phrase "a master among his people" [:4] means that the husband may not bury his wife. However, we know the law as the Sages have transmitted it: a kohen *does* bury his wife (the Sages used the word "his nearest kin" as a means of deriving this exegetically [Yevamot 22b], as I explained in the case of "to other people" [Exodus 21:8]). Furthermore, the word "master" denotes not a husband, but a man of substance, with many people in his household (as in, "its master was not with it" [Exodus 22:13]). Therefore, the original explanation must be invalid. ¶ **His mother** is mentioned before the father, because normally the male of the

defile himself. [4]A master may not defile himself for his household, and thereby become unholy. [5]They will not make their heads bald; they will not shave the corners of their beards; they will not make an incision in their flesh. [6]They will be consecrated to their God, so that they will not desecrate the Name of their God, for they offer up the fire-offering of GOD, the bread of their God — they will be holy. [7]They will not take a harlot woman or a profaned woman. They will not take a woman divorced by her husband. For he is consecrated to his God. [8]You must keep him holy, for he offers the bread of your God. He shall be

---

species outlives the female. [3] **who is near to him** i.e., a full sister, with whom he shares both a father and a mother. [4] Thus, **a master may not defile himself for his household** whether his people be kohanim or ordinary Israelites, except for the abovementioned relatives. **and thereby become unholy** This is an infinitive of the *nif'al* form. The *lamed* acquires a *dagesh* because it absorbs a second *lamed.* [5] **they will not make their heads bald** as a sign of mourning. **they will not shave the corners of their beards** as a sign of mourning — for such is the custom in certain areas in Chaldea. The surrounding context here explains the previously-given commandment regarding "...the corners of your beard" [20:27]. **incision** [*singular*] that is, not even one. The whole of Israel has already received these commandments [20:27]; but Scripture admonishes the kohanim in particular, to teach us that someone who *does* shave his head, or his beard, or cut his flesh, may not minister before GOD. [6] **so that they will not desecrate the Name of their God** which they are liable to do when they **offer up the fire-offering of GOD.** [7] **a harlot** In all of Scripture we find no instance where the plain meaning of this word is anything other than the literal one — even in the case of "they have given a boy for a harlot" [Joel 4:3], as I have explained. **a profaned woman** but less flagrant than a harlot. According to the plain meaning of the text, it is evident from the words of Ezekiel [Ezekiel 44:22] that a kohen *may* marry a widow — at least the widow of another kohen. Thus, the words of the tradition [Qiddushin 78b] are correct. [8] **You must keep him**

holy to you, for I, GOD, sanctify you, Who am holy. [9]The daughter of a kohen who desecrates herself to be a harlot — it is her father she desecrates: She will be burned with fire.

[10]The kohen greater than his brothers, upon whose head the oil of anointment was poured, and who has been consecrated to wearing the garments, will neither let the hair of his head grow nor will he rend his clothes. [11]Unto any dead people he must not enter. He must not defile himself

---

holy In your thoughts and in your speech. **the bread of your God** i.e., the food which is offered before GOD. **I, GOD, sanctify you** [*plural*] i.e., I sanctify *all* of you. **[9] desecrates herself** [Hebrew: *teḥel*] Many people say that this word comes from "beginning" [Hebrew: *tḥilla*]; but I believe it comes from "desecration" [Hebrew: *ḥillul*], except that here the word is in the *hif'il* form, as in "he may not break his word" [Numbers 30:3]. Both opinions require the word to stem from an *'ayin-'ayin* root, ḥ-l-l. The word, however, is irregular; and it seems likely that the reason for the irregularity, both in the infinitive *haḥel* [the *heh* is vocalized with a *pataḥ* instead of a *qammaṣ* — Translator] as well as in this word *teḥel* (where the *tav* is vocalized with a *ṣereh*), is to avoid confusion with "beginning", the other meaning of the root. Compare, "that it should not be profaned" [Hebrew: *heḥel*] [Ezekiel 20:9]. **the daughter...of a kohen** who desecrates herself through unchastity — since she has desecrated her father's honor — **she will be burned** (but only if she was married or betrothed).

[10] the garments i.e., the holy garments **he will neither let the hair of his head grow, nor will he rend his clothes** from this verse we can derive the laws of mourning, which the Sages, of blessed memory, have transmitted to us. **[11] any dead** [*masculine singular*] **people** [*feminine plural*] i.e., the dead *corpse* of any people. The word "corpse" [*masculine singular*] is implied, since "dead" is here used as an adjective. Compare, "the rich man answers with impudent [words]" [Proverbs 18:23] and "their food [*masculine*] is a goodly [*feminine*] [lamb]" [Habakkuk 1:16], where the word

for his father or for his mother. [12]He must not leave the Sanctuary. He must not desecrate the Sanctuary of his God, for he has upon him the crown of his God's anointment-oil: I am GOD. [13]He shall marry a woman in her virginity. [14] A widow, a divorcée, a profaned woman, a harlot — these he shall not marry, for only a virgin from his people may he take as a wife [15]that he not disqualify his children within his people. I am GOD, Who consecrates him.

"lamb" is implied. **he must not enter** into the tent or the house where the corpse lies: not even **for his father or for his mother**, whom he is obligated to honor in their lifetime and in their death, and certainly not for his brother or his son. **[12] He must not leave the Sanctuary** The Exegetes correctly interpreted this verse [Sanhedrin 18a] to mean: He will not leave the Sanctuary to follow the funeral procession. Some people interpret the verse literally, and apply it to the seven days of consecration; but this is implausible, because Scripture explicitly discusses the kohen who already "has been consecrated" [:10].[1] **[13] in her virginity** Certain nouns in the Holy Tongue are never singular, like "youth" [Isaiah 54:6], "old age" [Genesis 37:3], "girlhood" [*cf.* Isaiah 54:4], and "virginity" (likewise, certain nouns are never plural, like "young children" [Esther 3:13], "shoulders" [Genesis 9:23], "gold" [Genesis 24:22], and "iron" [Numbers 35:16]). **[14] a widow, a divorcée** whether from a kohen, or from a non-kohen. **a profaned woman, [or] a harlot** Scripture omits the connective *vav*, as in "the sun [and] the moon stood still" [Habakkuk 3:11]. Scripture repeats the restriction **only a virgin** in order to add the qualification **of his people**. He is forbidden to marry a virgin prisoner of war, or a virgin convert. **[15] He must not disqualify his children** by having sexual relations in secret with a widow, or a divorcée. Thus far, he had only been told not to *marry* such women in public.

---

[1]It is also plausible that, in any event, he should not leave the Sanctuary except when engaged in the fulfillment of a precept.

[16] GOD told Moshe: [17]Tell Aaron: "Anyone of your descendants throughout their generations who has within him a defect — he must not approach to offer the food of his God. [18]For anyone who has a defect within him will not approach: a blind man, or lame, or sunken-nosed, or stretch-legged, [19]or a man who has a broken leg or a broken arm, [20]or eyebrowless, or dwarf, or with a cataract in his eye, or scabies, or a boil, or inflated testis — [21]Any one with a physical defect, among the descendents of Aaron, must not approach to offer up the fire-offerings of GOD; he has a defect; he will not approach to offer up the bread of his God. [22]He may eat the food of his God, of

---

[16] After discussing the holiness of the kohanim, Scripture now lists disqualifying physical defects. The upcoming passage deals with the common kohanim, **[17]** therefore Scripture specifically includes anyone who is descended from Aaron. **the food of his God** denotes any sacrifice offered upon the Altar. **[18] sunken-nosed** the opposite of "stretched"; from ḥ-r-m, meaning "extinguish". **stretch-legged** from "to stretch himself" [Isaiah 28:20]. **[20] eyebrowless** An adjective, related to "high-peaked hills" [Psalms 68:17]. The *nun* forms part of the triliteral root. **dwarf** This word is to be taken literally: i.e., short in stature. **cataract** [Hebrew: *tevallul*] Some say the word denotes destruction, as in "they performed a destructive perversion" [Hebrew: *tevel*] [20:12]. Others relate the word to "mixed [Hebrew: *belula*] with oil" [2:5]. The *tav* is extraneous according to both explanations. **scabies** This also denotes an eye ailment, in many people's opinion. **boil** in the sense of "stuck together", as in "Samson gripped" [Judges 16:29]. Others understand the word in the sense of "contortion", as in "the man was startled, and turned over" [Ruth 3:8]. The *yod* is extraneous, like the *yod* in "oil" [Numbers 18:12]. **inflated** an adjective, from "wind". **testis** i.e., testicle. **[21]** After giving specifics, Scripture now states the general rule of **any one with a physical defect**. The phrase **he has a defect** is rhetorical, like "he cursed his father or his mother" [20:9]. **[22] the food of his God** The show-bread, the guilt-offering, and the sin-offering, all of

the most holy, and of the holy. [23]But he may not approach the Partition, nor may he approach the altar, because there is a defect within him. He must not desecrate My holy places, for I am GOD, Who sanctifies them." [24]Moshe spoke to Aaron and to his sons, and to all the Children of Israel.

[22:1]GOD told Moshe: [2]Tell Aaron and his sons that they must distance themselves from the sacred things of the Children of Israel; they must not desecrate My holy Name, that which they consecrate to Me. I am GOD. [3]Tell them: "Throughout your generations, any man who approaches — among all your descendents — the holy things that the Children of Israel consecrate to GOD while his ritual impurity is upon him, that soul will be cut off from before me: I am GOD. [4]Any man of Aaron's descen-

---

which are most holy compared to the peace-offering, which is also holy. **and of the holy** such as the tithes, and the firstborn animals. **[23] But he may not approach the Partition** if he is the High Priest; and he may also not approach **the altar**. **[24]** These laws were told to **all the Children of Israel** so that they would not allow a blemished kohen to perform a peace-offering for them (although there are other services which tradition permits such a kohen to perform).

[22:1] Having mentioned that a kohen with a defect may not eat holy food, Scripture now proceeds to warn the eater that he must also be ritually pure. **[2] they must distance themselves** as in, "you will keep disassociated" [15:31] — meaning, to detach himself, in order to draw appropriate distinctions. The verb is in the *nif'al* form, and comes from "Nazirite" [*cf. comment on* 25:5]. **and not desecrate** The verb takes a compound object: **they must not desecrate My holy name**, and they must not desecrate **that which they consecrate to Me. I am GOD** Who am holy. **[3] cut off from before Me; I am GOD** Whatever is cut off from GOD cannot continue to exist, as I have explained in an earlier place dealing

dants who has *ṣara'at*, or who suffers from a constant flow will not eat of the holy things, until he becomes ritually pure, as well as somone who touches any ritual impurity of the soul, or a man who has a seminal emission, [5]or a man who touches any creeping being which renders ritual impurity to it, or with a man who renders him ritually impure with any ritual impurity of his. [6]Someone who touches it will be ritually impure until the evening. He will not eat from the holy things unless he washes his flesh in the water. [7]When the sun sets he will be ritually pure. Afterward, he may eat from the holy things, because it is his bread. [8]He must not eat an animal that died by itself, or an animal that was torn, to become ritu-

---

with the mysteries of GOD. **[4] until he becomes ritually pure** after whatever number of days are appropriate in the particular case. **[5] which renders ritual impurity to it** i.e., which renders ritual purity *because of* it. Compare, "say for my sake [literally: to me], 'He is my brother'" [Genesis 20:13]. ¶All of the abovementioned events render one ritually impure until evening. **[7] When the sun sets he will be ritually pure** The subject of this sentence is obviously the abovementioned ritually impure man (compare, "the kohen will make an atonement for her, and she will be ritually pure" [12:8]). The word "day" is nowhere mentioned in the verse. However, our Sages, of blessed memory, have handed down the law that he should not eat food until *dark* (even after sunset), and they used this verse as a mnemonic by saying "the day clears away" [literally: the day becomes pure] [Berakhot 2a]. See my comment on the passage "to other people" [Exodus 21:8] for a similar device [the reference is to an earlier commentary on Exodus, known as the *Perush Haqqaṣar* – Translator]. **his bread** i.e., his food, as I have explained elsewhere [*comment on* Exodus 16:4]. **[8]** Certain brainless people have misinterpreted the verse in Ezekiel that reads "The kohanim shall not eat of anything that dies of itself, or is torn, whether it be bird or beast" [Ezekiel 44:31]. They claim that the prohibition applies only to food killed *by* birds or by beasts. This is nonsense. The Torah explicitly says, **he must not**

ally impure thereby: I am GOD. [9]They will observe my charge, and not thereby sin, and not die thereby, for they shall have desecrated it. I am GOD, Who sanctifies them. [10]A stranger must not eat that which is holy. An inhabitant of a kohen and an employee will not eat that which is holy. [11]If a kohen buys a person, he is an acquisition of his money: he may eat of it. One born of his household — they may eat his food. [12]A kohen's daughter who marries a strange man — she may not eat of the holy heave-offering. [13]A kohen's daughter who becomes a widow or divorcée, and has no progeny, and returns to her father's house, as in her youth — she may eat of her father's food; but no stranger may eat of it. [14]A man who erroneously eats that which is holy must add a fifth of its value together with it; he must give it to the kohen as hallowed food. [15]They must not desecrate the holy things of the Children of Israel, which they elevate to GOD. [16]They

---

eat an animal that died by itself, or an animal that was torn — i.e., *any* such animal. This verse teaches us that if he does eat such food, he may not officiate. **[9] They will observe My charge** [*feminine*] This alludes to the Sanctuary [*masculine*]. The verse accordingly continues: **and not thereby** [*masculine*] **sin, and not die thereby** [*masculine*]. **[10] a stranger** someone not descended from Aaron. **[11] they** [*masculine plural*] **may eat his food** both the men and the women. **[12] the holy heave-offering** the thigh and the breast [*cf.* 7:34]. **[13] she may eat of her father's food** just as she could originally. **but no stranger may eat of it** If she has a child, both she and the child fall under the category of **stranger**. She may not eat her father's food, on account of the child. **[14] he must give it to the kohen as hallowed food** This phrase might be interpreted, "*with* the hallowed food". Another possibility is that the verb in the phrase **he must give it to the kohen** takes a compound object, and that "it" refers back to **a fifth of its value**: He will give it to the kohen, *and* he will give the value of the hallowed food. In my opinion neither interpretation is necessary, because the word **to-**

will incur a sin of guilt upon them when they eat their holy things, for I am GOD Who sanctifies them."

[17]GOD told Moshe: [18]Tell Aaron, his sons, and all the Children of Israel, and say to them: "Any man of the House of Israel or a resident alien in Israel, who brings his offering for any of their vows or any of their pledges, which they may offer to GOD as a burnt-offering, [19]will be favorable to you. It shall be an unblemished male of the oxen, of the sheep, or of the goats. [20]You shall not bring whatever has a defect within it; it shall not be favorable to you. [21]If a man offers a peace-offering to GOD to express a vow or pledge — of oxen, or of the flock — it shall be unblemished, to be favorable. It must have no defect within it. [22]Blind, or broken, or split, or a wart, or scabies, or a boil — you shall not offer any such animal to GOD, nor will you place any of them on the altar as a

---

gether with it supplies the appropriate meaning. **[16] they will incur sin upon others** This transitive verb takes both a direct and an indirect object. The kohanim must instruct the people, so that they do not err.

[17] Scripture continues the general topic of the sacrificial offerings, now telling us that a blemished animal may not be sacrificed. **[18] or a resident alien** The laws concerning vows and pledges apply equally to Israel and to aliens, as it is written [Numbers 15:16]. Our Sages have distinguished between a "vow" and a "pledge" [Qinnim 1:1]. Every vow eventually becomes a pledge, but not every pledge ultimately becomes a vow. **[20]** Any offering which is entirely burnt upon the Altar should be entirely perfect. **[21] to express** i.e., to specify. **[22] blind** This is a feminine adjective, modifying the implied noun "eye". **Split** is related to the verb in "so be your judgment; you have selected it" [I Kings 20:40] and means "divided" (some people say that **broken** denotes the arm, whereas **split** denotes the leg). **wart** [Hebrew: *yabbelet*] as

fire-offering to GOD. [23]An ox or a lamb that is stretched-legged, or drawn in — you may make it a pledge, but as a vow it will not be acceptable. [24]Distorted, or crushed, or torn, or cut, you shall not offer to GOD, and in your domain you shall not do it. [25]From a foreigner you shall not offer any of these as the bread of your God: Their deformity is within them; there is a defect in them; they will not be acceptable for you."

[26]GOD told Moshe: [27]When an ox, or a sheep, or a goat will be born, it will stay with its mother the first week. From the eighth day onwards, it will be acceptable as an

---

in "cataract" [Hebrew: *tevallul*] [21:20]. ¶After all is said and done, we have no choice but to accept the traditional interpretation of these words [Bekhorot, Chapters 6 and 7], and not try to rely upon our limited understanding. **you shall not offer any such animal to GOD** You shall not specify such an animal as the fulfillment of a vow; and if already specified, you shall not sacrifice it. **[23] drawn in** [Hebrew: *qaluṭ*] is the opposite of **stretch-legged** (see above [21:18]) and is related to "a city of refuge" [Hebrew: *miqlaṭ*] [Joshua 21:13]. **[24] distorted** from "their breasts were pressed" [Ezekiel 23:3]. **crushed** from "I ground it into small bits" [Deuteronomy 10:21]. Both this term and the previous one refer to the testicles. **torn** from "as is broken a thread of tow" [Judges 16:9] **and in your domain you shall not do it** i.e., you shall not alter GOD's handiwork. **[25] from a foreigner** You may not rationalize, "Since the offering is from a foreigner, I need not be fastidious about it". **their deformity** [Hebrew: *moshḥatam*] from "corruption". The *mem* is extraneous, and the *tav* is part of the triliteral root; in the word "their anointing" [Hebrew: *moshḥatam*] [Exodus 40:15] the *mem* is part of the triliteral root, and the *tav* is extraneous. **acceptable** a verb in the *nif'al* form. Not only is this sacrifice **not acceptable**,

[27] but any animal younger than eight days old is also not acceptable. **an ox, a sheep, or a goat** either

• Scripture uses the names they will have after they are

offering to be consumed by fire for GOD. [28]Whether cattle or sheep — you shall not slaughter him and his son on the same day. [29]When you slaughter a thanksgiving-offering for GOD, that it be favorable to you when you shaughter it — [30]on that day it will be eaten. Do not leave any of it until morning: I am GOD. [31]Keep My commandments and practice them: I am GOD. [32]Do not desecrate My holy Name, and I shall be sanctified among

---

grown. Compare "you strip the naked of their clothing" [Job 22:6], "the dead man will be put to death" [Deuteronomy 17:6], and "a falling person may fall" [Deuteronomy 22:8].

or

- these terms denote the entire species.

from the eighth day like a baby being circumcised, the animal must be at least one week old. **onwards** i.e., *after*wards. This is borne out by the reappearance of the same word concerning Jonathan's arrow [I Samuel 20:37]. **[28] cattle or sheep** both male and female animals (see above [*comment on* 11:6]) are included in this commandment. **[29] When you slaughter a thanksgiving-offering** which must be eaten in a single day, as opposed to a parent and a child, which may *not* be slaughtered in a single day. This passage adds the word **favorable to you** to that which was previously stated in the *parasha* of *Ṣav* [7:15]. **[30] I am GOD** for Whom the thanksgiving-offering should be perfect. **[31] Keep My commandments** in your thoughts **and practice them; I am GOD** Who can probe all thoughts, and see all deeds. **[32]** It is evident from context that the commandment **Do not desecrate My holy Name** is addressed to the descendants of Aaron. They are the ones whom Scripture enjoins not to slaughter a mother and a child on the same day [:28], whether for themselves or for the Israelites. They are probably also the ones to whom the commandment "When you slaughter a thanksgiving-offering..." [:29] is addressed. The fact that the next passage begins with "Tell the children of Israel" [23:2] supports the proposition that the current passage is *not* addressed to the children of Israel. Moreover, the phrase **I shall be sanctified among the children of Israel** refers to the Israelites in

the Children of Israel. I am GOD, Who hallows you,
[33]Who took you out of the land of Egypt to be your God;
I am GOD.

[23:1]GOD told Moshe: [2]Tell the Children of Israel, and say
to them: "The times chosen by GOD which you will declare as holy occasions — these are My chosen times:
[3]For six days work will be done; on the seventh day is a
Sabbath of complete rest, a holy occasion; you will do no
work. It is a Sabbath to GOD in all your settlements.

[4]These are the times chosen by GOD, holy occasions

---

the third person. [33] **Who took you out ... I am GOD** This is the first of the Ten Commandments, and the underlying principle behind all the others.

[23:1] After dealing with the sacrifices, Scripture proceeds to mention the days on which the children of Israel will offer burnt-offerings, beginning with the Sabbath. [2] **these are My chosen times** Scripture employs the plural because there are many Sabbaths in a year [*cf.* :4]. [3] **it is a Sabbath to GOD** see above [*comment on* Exodus 16:23]. **in all your settlements** both within your land, and outside your land; both at home, and on the road.

[4] Scripture now discusses festivals. The Sabbaths were called "*My* chosen times" [:2]; the festivals are called **their chosen time**, because GOD does not determine the day of the week on which they fall. Allow me at this point to present a few general principles concerning the festivals. ¶In the days when the Temple still stood, the Sanhedrin determined when the festivals would be held. Consider the case of King Hezekiah's Passover, where Scripture clearly

says "The king had taken counsel..." [II Chronicles 30:2].[1] The Exegetes tell us that the Sanhedrin would examine many factors when determining the length of the year. For example, Rabbi 'Aqiba is said to have decreed two [actually three — Translator] leap years in a row [Sanhedrin 12a], because the situation required it. ¶In all of Scripture we find no evidence of the procedure whereby ancient Israel maintained its calendar. Sa'adya Ga'on claims that they made the calendar conform to the same fixed rules that we now employ; but this cannot be true, as the Mishna and the Talmud both record that Passover occasionally used to fall on Monday, Wednesday, or Friday. Two stories tell of the occurrence of such events. Today we add a leap month whenever the lunar year falls approximately one month behind the solar year, but in ancient times this was not the case. ¶The Jewish calendar began on a Friday morning at 8 o'clock (by adding 4 days, 8 hours, 48 minutes and 40 seconds to Sunday night, 11 minutes and 20 seconds past 11 o'clock in the evening, we get 8 o'clock Friday morning[2]), and the first intercalation occurred one and a half years later. Nowadays, the calendar is based on the average duration of the moon's orbit. Although the interval between two *appearances* of the new moon is "sometimes longer and sometimes shorter" [Rosh HaShana 25a] than a lunar month, the actual sighting of the moon over Jerusalem (or over any other place) does not occasion the declaration of the new month. To prove this, assume that the midpoints of the sun, moon, and earth are all connected by a straight line. Is Jerusalem necessarily the place where this line intersects the earth's surface? Moreover, whenever we see the new moon of Nisan on a Sunday night — and everyone around the world see the new moon at the same time — the month of Nisan does not begin until Monday

---

[1] Our Sages, of blessed memory, took issue with this action, because a leap month was inserted after the new moon of Nisan had been announced. It is not proper to lengthen a year once Nisan has occurred by inserting a second Nisan [Sanhedrin 12b].

[2] Year 1 of the calendar is imagined to have begun at Sunday night, 11 minutes and 20 seconds past 11 o'clock in the evening, even though Year 1 actually consisted only of the five days which preceded the creation of mankind. A single day would be sufficient to require the counting of a new year. We need not concern ourselves with the difference between the solar Year 1 and the lunar Year 1, since the year never existed anyway and is only a harmless mathematical convenience.

which you will declare in their chosen time. [5]In the first month, on the fourteenth of the month, in the afternoon, is the Passover to GOD. [6]On the fifteenth day of this

---

night. The months of Ṭevet, Shvaṭ, and 'Adar can likewise be delayed one day after the sighting of the new moon. This can happen whenever the New Year is delayed two days, because the new moon of Tishrey falls on Tuesday morning, after 03:11:20. There are also occasions when the month of Tishrey begins on Thursday, but the moon remains invisible even as late as Friday night and even if the sky is clear: Whenever the new moon occurs close to midday, the strong light of the sun renders it invisible, because the new moon is always in the same part of the sky as the sun. Even the astronomical moment when the moon is directly between the sun and the earth does not always determine the start of a new month. In particular, the New Year following a leap year is always postponed one day whenever this moment occurs on a Monday morning, after 09:38:16$^{2}/_{3}$. It is also postponed, as was mentioned earlier, when the moment of collinearity occurs on a Tuesday morning, after 03:11:20. Were it not for my unwillingness to digress, I would explain the mysteries of intercalation, and the little-understood laws regarding a new moon that occurs before midday. The main point is that our Sages, of blessed memory, have transmitted to us the law that in Exile we are to base our calendar completely on a fixed set of rules. This tradition dates back to the time of the prophets, and we cannot improve upon it. ¶The practice of observing two-day festivals in the lands of Exile originally arose because of uncertainty over when the month began. Nowadays some people fast two days on Yom Kippur, in order to conform both to the calculated New Moon and to the astronomical New Moon. Such fasting does them no good, however, because the New Year is often delayed two days after the new moon appears. Suppose a month "ought" to begin with the new moon. Whenever the new moon of Tishrey occurs on Tuesday morning, after 03:11:20, then they "ought" to fast on the eighth day of Tishrey. Thus, why should we subvert the rules which have been handed down to us, for the sake of creating an entirely different calendar? — for that is what will happen if we conform our calendar to the sighting of the new moon. **[5] in the afternoon** see

month is the Festival of Maṣṣot, to GOD: You will eat maṣṣot for seven days. [7]You will have a holy occasion on the first day: You will do no servile work. [8]You will offer a fire-offering to GOD for seven days. On the seventh day is a holy occasion: You will do no servile work."

[9]GOD told Moshe: [10]Speak to the Children of Israel and tell them: "When you come to the land I give you, and you reap its harvest, you shall bring an 'omer of the first of your harvest to the kohen. [11]He will wave the 'omer before GOD so that it will be favorable for you; from the

---

above [*comment on* Exodus 12:6] [8] Scripture will give the details of the **fire-offering** in the *parasha* of *Pinḥas* [Numbers 28:19].

[10] The phrase **when you come to the land** is not mentioned until now, because we had to keep the Sabbath even in the wilderness (which is why the passage dealing with the Sabbath [Exodus 35:2-3] appears next to the passage dealing with the Tabernacle), and because we observed one Passover at Mount Sinai. **speak to the Children of Israel** for them to assemble; and then, **tell them** the following: **[11] the day after the day of rest** [literally: the day after the Sabbath] Our Sages, of blessed memory, have said [Menaḥot 65b] that this denotes the second day of the festival; the Dissenters maintain that the verse should be taken literally. The faithful bring examples from the Sabbatical Year [25:2], the Jubilee, Yom Kippur [:32], and the New Year [:24], all of which are called "sabbath". The first and the eighth days of Sukkot are called "sabbath" [:39], too [*see also comment on* Exodus 31:13]. Moreover, a "sabbath" also means a "week", as in "seven sabbaths" [:15] as well as "those who came in on the Sabbath, along with those who had finished for the week" [II Kings 11:9] (where one verse uses two different meanings of the same word[1]). ¶In addition to these definitive arguments, Meshullam ben Qalonymus

[1]Another verse that uses a word in two different ways is "He had thirty sons that rode on thirty donkey-colts [Hebrew: *'ayarim*] and they had thirty cities [Hebrew: *'ayarim*] ..." [Judges 10:4].

of Rome attempted to bring a proof from "...on the day after the Passover, maṣṣot and toasted grain" [Joshua 5:11] without realizing that he thereby weakened his own argument. The Passover sacrifice occurs on the fourteenth of the month; the day after the Passover sacrifice is the *first* day of the festival, as it is written: "They marched from Rameses, in the first month, on the fifteenth day of the first month, the day after the Passover" [Numbers 33:3]. However, the eating of parched grain is forbidden until after the 'Omer-offering has been waved! To resolve this, Sa'adya Ga'on proposed

1) that there are *two* Passovers: the first is Israel's Passover, while the second is GOD's Passover, and is observed on the evening of the fifteenth. Thus, the reference to "the day after Passover" in Joshua is a reference to the sixteenth of the month, but the reference to "the day after Passover" in the Torah denotes the day after the Passover *sacrifice.* This explanation is unsatisfactory, because the Passover festival owes its name to GOD's passing over our houses. "The day after" that event denotes the following morning — which is still the fifteenth (compare, "...the entire day, the entire night, and the entire day after" [Numbers 11:32]).
2) Sa'adya Ga'on also suggested that the "maṣṣot and toast" were from the previous year's crop, which makes sense. Scripture says that the waving of the 'Omer offering takes place "from the time when you begin to reap the grain" [Deuteronomy 16:9]. If the waving of the 'Omer that year occurred on the fifteenth, when did they have time to harvest the grain and prepare maṣṣot? Even if they had had the time, the only harvest so far that year was the beginning of the barley crop. The choice of words is also suggestive: Scripture says, "from the land through which they had passed [Hebrew: *'avur*]" [Joshua 5:11]; the word may have been used because it describes the produce from the year that had just passed [Hebrew: *'avra*] ("the land through which they had passed" literally means the land of Siḥon and 'Og). This is borne out by the contrasting phrase, "...from the fresh produce

> of the land of Canaan" [Joshua 5:12]. Besides, "toast" [Hebrew: *qaluy*] is not the same thing as "parched grain" [Hebrew: *qalee*]. Scripture states only that "You will eat neither bread, nor parched grain [Hebrew: *qalee*], nor kernels" [:14]. The verse "ripe ears toasted [Hebrew: *qaluy*] in fire" [2:14] does not contradict anything we have said, because there the word *qaluy* is used as an adjective. Anything which is "toasted" in fire can be called "toast".

We may press the question still further: What grounds have we to assume that the kohen waved the 'Omer offering as soon as they crossed the Jordan? In fact, the verse distinctly says "the land which I give you" [:10] and the land as yet had not been given to them. The entire point of the verse in question is that the manna stopped; Scripture mentions the maṣṣot and the toast only in the context of the stopping of the manna. ¶Sa'adya Ga'on also pointed out, that if we are to take the word "Sabbath" literally, from *which* Sabbath are we to begin the count? Rabbi Abu al-Faraj Furqan ibn Asad replied that there are eighteen days called "set times", besides the Sabbath, when an additional sacrifice is offered [Numbers, Chapters 28 and 29]. Since we know that an additional sacrifice is offered on the day the 'Omer is waved [:12], we can deduce that the day of the 'Omer waving must be included in the days of the Spring festival. He seems to have forgot, however, that the New Month sacrifices are also not mentioned in the list! Moreover, Scripture says, "These shall be offered each day for seven days" [Numbers 28:24]. According to him, it should say, "...except for the day on which the 'Omer-waving falls" (the absence of such a phrase poses no problem for *us*, though, because we derive the Commandments from the oral tradition). The *parasha* of *Pinḥas* also does not discuss the lambs of the peace-offering [*cf.* :19] when it comes to the festival of Shavu'ot, nor does it say anything about the "one young ox, and two rams" mentioned in the previous verse [:18] — instead, it talks about "two ... bullocks, and one ram" [Numbers 28:27]. ¶The believer can also argue that Moshe knew prophetically that the first day of the month would be a Sabbath, and consequently he would know on what day of the week the 'Omer waving would fall (just as he would know that the first arrangement of the showbread would occur on a Sabbath [24:8] [*comment on* Exodus 40:2]). Scripture mentions the days on which

day after the day of rest the kohen will wave it. [12]On the day you wave the Omer, you will offer an unblemished yearling he-lamb as a burnt-offering to GOD. [13]Its cereal-offering will be two-tenths of fine flour mixed with oil, a fire-offering to GOD that is willingly accepted. The wine-offering will be a quarter of a *hin*. [14]You will eat neither bread, nor parched grain, nor kernels, until that very day, until you bring the offering of your God. This is an everlasting decree throughout your generations, in all your settlements.

---

events fell during the first year; but subsequent years use the terms "your Festival of Weeks" [Numbers 28:26] and "seven weeks" [Deuteronomy 16:9] rather than speaking in terms of "Sabbaths" [:15]. Similarly, in the first year they offered the sacrifices mentioned here; but in subsequent years they offered the sacrifices in the *parasha* of *Pinḥas.* ¶It is useless to say that a "week" perforce begins on Sunday. The phrase "she will be ritually impure for two weeks" [12:5] clearly invalidates such an argument. ¶Most people do not realize that the reason why Scripture does not mention the day on which Shavu'ot falls — alone among all the festivals — is that we are commanded to *count* to the day of the festival. Our Sages, of blessed memory, said [Shabbat 86b] that the day on which Shavu'ot falls is the anniversary of the giving of the Torah, and that the statement "we have a festival of GOD" [Exodus 10:9] is a reference to Shavu'ot. **favorable** Some people always translate this as "acceptable". In other words, **He will wave the 'Omer before GOD so that it will be acceptable for you** — i.e., you wave it for Him to accept it from you. Similarly, **[12]** you shall offer a **yearling** lamb, in order that you may be found acceptable. The Dissenters claim that **yearling** does not mean "a year old" [*cf. comment on* 12:6]. The former, according to them, denotes an animal under one year of age, whereas the latter denotes an animal one year old or older. The passage dealing with the dedication of the Altar, however, speaks of "one yearling lamb" [Numbers 7:15], yet in the end gives a total count of "twelve one-year lambs" [Numbers 7:87]. **[14] bread** from the new crop is forbidden (for the Passover sacrifice is to be eaten "with maṣṣot and bitter herbs"

[15]You will count for yourselves from the day after the day of rest, from the day you bring the 'omer of the wave-offering; seven complete weeks will there be. [16]Until the day after the seventh week you shall count fifty days, and you will offer a new cereal-offering to GOD. [17]From your settlements you will bring bread for waving: there will be two, of two-tenths of fine flour, baked leavened — a first-fruit offering to GOD. [18] You will offer with the bread seven unblemished yearling he-lambs, one bull of the herd, and two rams. They will be a burnt-offering to GOD, and their cereal-offering and drink-offerings, an offering consumed by fire, willingly accepted by GOD. [19]You will make one he-goat into a sin-offering,

---

[Numbers 9:11]).

[15] Were it not for the tradition, we would think that the counting of the days of the 'Omer resembles the counting of the years until Jubilee. The Dissenters explain **complete** to mean that we should not count the first Sabbath, but rather that the counting should begin with the day immediately following. **[16] you shall count fifty days** In Biblical Hebrew, the number given always includes both the first and the last days of the count. Similarly, Scripture always means one week when it uses the phrase "on the eighth day" [e.g., 12:3]. **[17] you will bring** The *dagesh* in the *'alef* is peculiar, and no one knows why it is there. **from your settlements** We depend on the tradition [Menaḥot 83b] to elucidate from where the wheat must come, and when it should be offered. **bread for waving** The kohen receives this, along with the lambs of the peace offering [*cf.* :20]. **[18]** It seems that Scripture deviated in the first year from the sacrifices prescribed for subsequent years — probably because the first year marked the inauguration of the sacrificial system. Others say that the kohen may bring either a **bull ... and two rams** or two oxen and "one ram" [Numbers 28:27], whichever he chooses. No other commandment, however, provides this kind of option. I shall explain the true meaning of the discrepancy in the *parasha* of *Pinḥas* [*comment on* Numbers

and two yearling he-lambs into peace-offerings. [20]The kohen will wave them with the bread of the first-fruit as a wave-offering before GOD, with the two lambs. They will be consecrated to GOD, belonging to the kohen. [21]You will declare this very day as a holy occasion for you: You will do no servile work. It is an everlasting decree in all your settlements throughout your generations. [22]When you reap the harvest of your land, do not complete the corner of your field as you reap, nor gather the fallen stalks of your harvest. Leave them for the poor and for the alien: I am GOD, your God."

[23]GOD told Moshe: [24]Tell the Children of Israel: "In the seventh month, on the first of the month, will be for you a day of rest, a remembrance of sounding the horn, a holy

---

28:27]. **[19]** Scripture authorizes us to slaughter peace-offerings on the holiday of Shavu'ot, which is a major festival. From here we derive the permissibility of slaughtering peace-offerings on *all* major festivals, contrary to the opinion of the Sadducees [a derogatory reference to Karaites – Translator]. **[22]** The commandment of **when you reap the harvest of your land** is mentioned a second time [*cf.* 19:9] apropos the festival of Shavu'ot, which involves the first-fruits of the wheat harvest. We must not forget the commandments which pertain to that time of year.

[23] The phrase **GOD told Moshe** introduces the section on Rosh HaShana, to stress that it is a festival in its own right (as opposed to Shavu'ot, which stems from the waving of the 'Omer). For the same reason, this phrase introduces the sections on Yom Kippur [:26] and the festival of Sukkot [:33]. **[24] the seventh month** The months are counted from Nisan, since that was when we left Egypt. Also, the barley ripening begins a new agricultural year, followed by "the first-fruits of the wheat harvest" [Exodus 34:22], and followed in turn by "when you gather your products" [Exodus 23:16]. Each of these festivals must be celebrated on its given day. ¶Since we normally blow trumpets every month

occasion. [25]You shall do no servile work, and you shall bring a fire-offering to GOD."

[26]GOD told Moshe: [27]However, on the tenth of this, the seventh month, is the Day of Atonement. It shall be for you a holy occasion, and you shall afflict yourselves. You will offer a fire-offering to GOD . [28] You will do no work on that very day, for it is a day of atonement, that atones for

---

[Numbers 10:10], this day is called **a remembrance of sounding the horn**. Elsewhere it is called "a day of sounding the horn" [Numbers 29:1], because on this day (as on Yom Kippur of the jubilee year [25:9]) there is a separate commandment to blow the ram's horn. Attend carefully now, and perhaps you shall understand the mysteries which I now reveal. The Exegetes have said that Rosh HaShana is the Day of Judgment, and that the ram's horn reminds us of GOD's majesty. Although every new month is heralded by the blowing of trumpets, the month of Nisan is preeminent over them all. On the first of Nisan the Tabernacle was erected; so it will also be in the future, as Ezekiel says: "in the first month, on the first day of the month" [Ezekiel 45:18]. He also says, "and so shall you do on the seventh day of the month" [Ezekiel 45:20] and on that day the sun and the moon are at right angles to one another. The festival on the fifteenth of Nisan occurs when the sun and the moon are directly opposite one another. The seventh day of the festival occurs when the sun and moon are again at right angles to one another. Accordingly, Rosh HaShana is the most important *day* of the year. Although it is a Day of Judgment, one may not fast on it, as Ezra showed us [Nehemiah 8:10]. Yom Kippur comes next, when the Moon is in conjunction with Aquarius, and then comes Sukkot, which is just like Passover except it has eight days instead of seven. Thus the mystery of the festivals and the mystery of the Sabbath are now clarified [not quite — Translator].

[27] Scripture says **However** concerning the holiday **on the tenth** because normally a holiday is a happy day. For example, in Ezra's book we see the phrase "go your way, eat sumptuously, and drink sweet beverages" [Nehemiah 8:10]. **you shall afflict your-**

you before GOD, your God. [29]Any person who is not afflicted on this very day will be cut off from his people, [30]and any person who does any work on this very day — I will cause that person to be lost from amid his people. [31]You shall do no work. This is an everlasting decree throughout your generations in all your settlements. [32] It is a Sabbath of Sabbath for you; you will afflict yourselves. On the ninth of the month in the evening, from evening to evening, you must keep your Sabbath.

[33]GOD told Moshe: [34]Tell the Children of Israel: "On the fifteenth day of this, the seventh month, is the Festival of Sukkot: seven days to GOD. [35]On the first day is a holy occasion; you shall do no servile work. [36]For seven days you shall present a fire-offering to GOD. On the eighth day will be a holy occasion for you, and you will bring a fire-offering to GOD. It is a stoppage: You will do no ser-

---

selves explained above [*comment on* 16:29]. **[28] that atones for you** This seemingly redundant phrase means: The day of atonement atones *only* for you. **[29] any person who is not afflicted** The verb is in the passive mood, and this teaches us that someone who is known not to observe this commandment properly must be compelled to fast. We may not labor, so that we will involve ourselves exclusively with repentance. **[30]** There is a difference between **I will cause to be lost** and "will be cut off" [:29], but I cannot explain it. **[31]** Scriptures states **you shall do no work** a second time in order to add the phrase **this is an everlasting decree throughout your generations....** **[32] keep your Sabbath** Compare this to the Sabbath day, which is not called Israel's Sabbath, but rather GOD's Sabbath [:3].

[36] for seven days you shall present a fire-offering Unlike the fire-offering of the Passover holiday, however, these fire-offerings are not all identical. **it is a stoppage** [Hebrew: *'aṣeret*] Some say this word means "assembly", as in "an assembly [Hebrew: *'aṣeret*] of

vile work. [37]These are GOD's chosen times, which you will declare holy occasions; to bring a fire-offering to GOD: burnt-offerings, grain-offerings, sacrifices and libations, as required for each day; [38]besides the Sabbaths of GOD, besides your gifts, besides all your vows and all your pledges which you will give to GOD. [39]However, on the fifteenth day of the seventh month, when you gather the produce of the land, you will celebrate GOD's festival for seven days; on the first day is a day of rest, and on the eighth day is a day of rest. [40]You shall lift up for yourselves on the first day, a fruit of the *hadar* tree, branches of date palms, a

---

treacherous men" [Jeremiah 9:1] — in that all Israel gathers together for the three festivals. This translation is incorrect, because concerning Passover Scripture says, "on the seventh day there will be an *'aṣeret*" [Deuteronomy 16:8]; yet earlier Scripture has said, "in the morning you may return to your homes" [Deuteronomy 16:7]. It is more plausible to translate the word along the lines of "detained [Hebrew: *ne'ṣar*] before GOD" [I Samuel 21:8] to denote a respite from wordly concerns. Accordingly, Scripture says, **it is a stoppage: you will do no servile work**. A similar phrase describes the stoppage on Passover. **[37] These are GOD's chosen times** whereon you are required to offer **a fire-offering**. All of the holidays involve **burnt-offerings, grain-offerings, sacrifices and libations**. Thus far only the term **fire-offering** has been mentioned; this term probably denotes either the burnt-offering or the grain-offering. **[38] your gifts** during the three festivals; and also vows (whether they be communal or individual); and also your pledges. **[39]** Since the previous passage discusses self-affliction, Scripture now uses the word **However** to teach us that it is forbidden to fast on Sukkot, as it is written: "you shall rejoice" [Deuteronomy 16:14] and "you shall be only happy" [Deuteronomy 16:15]. **when you gather the produce of the land** fields as well as vineyards **you will celebrate** This *'ayin-'ayin* verb refers to the festival peace-offering. **on the first day is a day of rest** The latter word is a predicate nominal; the connective "...there will be for you..." is implied (if the latter word were a predicate adjective, then the *heh*

**bough of a myrtle tree, and the brook-willow; and you
shall rejoice before GOD, your God, for seven days. [41]You
will celebrate it as a festival to GOD, seven days in the
year; it is a everlasting decree throughout your generations; in the seventh month you will celebrate it. [42]You
will dwell in the huts for seven days; every citizen within
Israel will dwell in the huts. [43]So that your generations
will know that I caused the children of Israel to dwell in
the huts when I took them out of the land of Egypt: I am**

---

of the definite article would replace the preposition *bet*). **[40] you shall lift up for yourselves** We translate according to the words of the Exegetes — since they do not contradict the plain meaning of Scripture — even though elsewhere we translate "every man shall acquire for himself a lamb, for the family group" [Exodus 12:3]. The Exegetes have also transmitted to us the tradition that the **fruit of the *hadar* tree** denotes the citron, and, in truth, there is no tree with fruit more beautiful [Hebrew: *hadar*]. They also called it "the fruit that resides [Hebrew: *haddar*] on its tree" as a kind of mnemonic [Sukka 35a], as I have explained above concerning the passage "to other people" [Exodus 21:8] [the reference is to an earlier commentary on Exodus, known as the *Perush Haqqaṣar* — Translator]. ¶The Sadducees [a derogatory reference to Karaites — Translator] have said that the Sukka must be built from these four species, bringing a proof from Ezra's book [Nehemiah 8:15]. Didn't these half-wits notice that no mention is made there of the **brook-willow**, nor of any kind of fruit? On the contrary, it is only a list of branches from five kinds of trees (the fact that "myrtle branches" are mentioned separately from "thick-tree branches" [Nehemiah 8:15] poses no problem to the traditional interpretation; there are two varieties — one tall and one short — and there the term "myrtle" denotes the short variety). **[43] in huts** After the crossing of the Red Sea they lived in booths (and did so even in the Sinai Desert, where they stayed for nearly a year), following the custom of all military camps. Any perceptive person who travels from Arabia to Edom will understand the reason for this commandment. This festival, like the others, commemorates the Exodus from Egypt. You might ask: Why must this commandment be ob-

GOD, your God." [44]Moshe spoke of GOD's chosen times to the children of Israel.

[24:1] GOD told Moshe: [2]Command the Children of Israel: "Bring for yourselves pure olive oil, beaten for illumination, to light the lamp always. [3]Outside the Partition of the Testimony, in the Tent of Assembly, Aaron will arrange it, from evening till morning before GOD, perpetually; it is an everlasting decree throughout your generations. [4]He will prepare the lights in the pure lamp before GOD perpetually.

[5]Take fine flour and bake in into twelve loaves; each loaf

---

served in Tishrey? One possible answer is that although GOD's clouds covered the camp during the day, and protected it from the sun, it was necessary to construct huts on account of the cold from the time of Tishrey onwards. **[44] to the children of Israel** not literally to *all* the children of Israel, since he could not possibly speak to all of them. The same applies whenever the phrase "speak to the children of Israel" appears. The verse "the entire assembly of the children of Israel" [19:2] poses no problem, since the term "assembly" does not denote the entire nation.

[24:2] After mentioning the holidays that require a fire-offering [23:37], Scripture must discuss the showbread [:5]. First, however, Scripture interposes the passage of **pure olive oil** because the Lamp stood directly opposite from the bread table. **[4]** In this passage Scripture inserts the phrase **in the pure lamp** to denote *the* lamp: i.e., the one Beṣal'el made of pure gold, and no other (the one made of iron in an emergency ['Avoda Zara 43a] was made at the express instruction of prophets[1]).

---

[1] [The *halakha* [Menaḥot 28a] is that the lamp can be made of any metal; there is also no evidence of prophetic activity in Hashmonean times — Translator]

will be two-tenths. [6]Set them in two tiers, six to a tier, on the pure table before GOD. [7]Put pure frankincense atop the tier. It will be for the bread as a memorial-part, a fire-offering to GOD. [8]He will arrange it perpetually before GOD, every Sabbath. It is from the Children of Israel, an everlasting covenant. [9]It will belong to Aaron and his family, and they will eat it in a hallowed place, for it is his most holy from GOD's fire-offerings, an eternal portion."

[10]The son of an Israelite woman came out (he was the son of an Egyptian man) amid the children of Israel. They quarreled in the camp — the son of the Israelitess,

---

[5] **Take fine flour** i.e., tell someone to take it. Similarly, **bake** also denotes an action to be done through an agent. The word **bake** is irregular, as it is accented on the ultima. The **two tenths** correspond to the [6] **two tiers**, with the total number of loaves corresponding to the number of tribes (like the Ephod [Exodus 28:9] and the Breastplate [Exodus 28:21]). **on the pure table** as opposed to other tables which might be there. Only this table was covered with gold, and had a golden crown [Exodus 25:24]. [7] The frankincense that was with the bread became a **fire-offering to GOD**; the bread itself belonged to the kohen. ¶This passage probably appears here because the community of Israel has a permanent obligation to offer the holiday burnt-offerings, as well as to supply oil and bread. [9] **to Aaron and his family** [literally: and his sons] i.e., to all the members of his household.

[10] There is no known reason why the upcoming passage is included here. Perhaps the blasphemer spoke inappropriately regarding the showbread, or the oil, or the sacrifices. **The son of an Israelite woman came out** from his tent. Compare, "they came out and stood at the entrance of their tents" [Numbers 16:27]. **the son of an Egyptian man** who had converted to Judaism. **[the] Israelite man** Scripture omits the definite article before the modified noun, as in "to [the] rich man" [II Samuel 12:4] and "[the] seventh day"

and the Israelite man. [11]The son of the Israelite woman pronounced the Name and cursed, and they brought him to Moshe. His mother's name was Shlomith, the daughter of Divri, of the tribe of Dan. [12]They set him in the prison, to specify for themselves by the word of GOD.

[13]GOD told Moshe: [14]Take the one who cursed outside the camp, and all the witnesses will lay their hands on his head; and the entire assembly will stone him. [15]Speak to the children of Israel, saying: "Whoever curses his Lord will bear his sin. [16]If he pronounces the Name of GOD, he will be killed; the entire assembly will stone him. Both the alien and the native shall be put to death for

---

[Genesis 2:3]. **[11] he pronounced** Some translate this word to mean "uttered", as in "which the mouth of GOD shall express" [Isaiah 62:2] and "as specified by name" [Numbers 1:17]. Others render it along the lines of "How shall I curse" [Numbers 23:8]. The former explanation strikes me as more plausible. **[12] in the prison** a portion of the campsite which had been so designated.

[14] all the witnesses will lay their hands... because someone may be stoned only by the testimony of witnesses. **[15]** Some people apply the phrase **who curses his Lord** to the case when someone blasphemes secretly. The truth of the matter is that "lord" is a common noun. Both angels [Judges 13:22] [*comment on* Genesis 3:5] and judges [Exodus 22:27] are called "lords". How can one know which meaning the blasphemer intended? However, **[16]** if he utters the Glorious Name, which is *not* a descriptive name, and cannot be mistaken for a common noun, then it can only denote Him and no one else [*cf. comment on* Exodus 3:15]. Thus the meaning of this verse is: When someone blasphemes, *if* he pronounces the Name, then he is put to death **for blaspheming the Name**. This is what happened in the case of the Egyptian's son. Notice that, out of respect for GOD, the passage on blasphemy does not mention the Name. **the entire assembly** meaning, the leaders of Israel. **both the alien and the native shall be put to death** This

blaspheming the Name. [17]A man who kills any other person will be put to death; [18]whoever strikes a beast will make restitution for it — a soul for a soul. [19]A man who gives an injury to his fellowman — as he has done, so shall be done to him: [20]a fracture for a fracture, an eye for an eye, a tooth for a tooth. As he gives an injury to

---

leads us to the upcoming passage, **[17]** which discusses assault (since the two men who fought, above, almost certainly struck one another). Although these laws were given before [Exodus 21:12*ff*], they are repeated here to add the phrase "for both the alien and the native" [:22]. We begin with the case of one who **kills any other person** deliberately (except in wartime), whether the victim be an alien or a native. **[18]** However, if he **strikes ... a beast** then he must only **make restitution**. The phrase **a life for a life** is thus used in two different senses to refer to each of the previous two verses. **[19] so shall be done to him** Compare Samson's words: "so have I done to them" [Judges 15:11] [where the term denotes equivalent, but not equal, compensation — Translator]. In addition, Sa'adya Ga'on has brought numerous other proofs, from simple common sense, that Scripture could not mean **[20] a fracture for a fracture** literally. For example, since the original wound was not precisely calculated, how could one duplicate it exactly? If not, and if the wound is in a sensitive area, one might kill the guilty party inadvertently! If someone removed one-third, say, of another person's eyelid, how could one possibly give the guilty party precisely that wound? Accordingly, the words of the tradition [Bava Qama 83b] must be correct. The true explanation in all these cases is that the guilty party *deserves* to lose an eye, but instead, he pays its monetary equivalent. If people should ask, "what if the guilty party is poor?" we answer that the law deals with the cases that are likely to occur. Besides, we can throw the question back at the questioners: What if the guilty party is blind? At least a poor person can conceivably become rich! **so it shall be given upon him** [literally: with him] [to "give upon" someone in Hebrew means to fine him — Translator]

- Often, the letter **bet** ["with"] takes the place of the preposition "upon". Compare, "upon [literally: with] which I rode" [Nehemiah 2:12]. Many other examples

his fellowman, so it shall be given upon him. [21]Whoever strikes a beast must render compensation for it. Whoever strikes a man must be put to death. [22]You must have one form of justice for an alien as for the native; for I am GOD, your God." [23]Moshe spoke to the children of Israel, and they took the blasphemer outside the camp, and stoned him. The children of Israel did as GOD had commanded Moshe.

---

exist.

or

- **so it shall be given in him** — i.e., so shall it be done to him — if he does not compensate his victim.

[21] One possible reason why the case of **Whoever strikes a beast** is here repeated, is to include the case when an alien is the victim. The laws of personal injury apply only within the nation of Israel (as it is written: "his fellowman" [:19]). However, when the case involves killing a person, or killing an animal, then [22] **you must have one form of justice for an alien as for the native** [literally: "like the alien, like the native"]. I have already explained that placing the two words "like" in parallel construction is a way of speaking concisely. Scripture also employs brevity in the previous verse by not mentioning "whoever strikes a man *and kills him* will be put to death". Such a qualifier is unnecessary, since it is obvious that the guilty party is not executed unless the victim dies. ¶Another possible explanation: Scripture first uses the term "strikes fatally" [:17] to describe someone who strikes a person in a sensitive area. Later, Scriptures gives the general principle that whoever kills another must be executed, whether he struck him in a sensitive area or not. That is why the second instance does not use the word "fatally". **your** [*plural*] **God** The God of the native and the God of the alien. [23] **The children of Israel did ...** From that day onwards, they enforced all the laws of personal injury.

[25:1] The Torah does not always follow chronological order. This passage was given before the *parasha* of *Vayyiqra* and the *parashiyyot* that follow it, since it was said **on Mount Sinai**. It con-

[25:1]GOD spoke to Moshe on Mount Sinai, saying: [2]Tell the Children of Israel: "When you come to the land I am giving you, the land shall be given a rest; it is the Sabbath of GOD. [3]Six years you may sow your field, and six years you may prune your vineyard; and you will gather in its produce; [4]but on the seventh year the land will have a Sabbath of Sabbath, a Sabbath of GOD. Neither sow your field, nor prune your vineyard. [5]You shall not reap the accretion of your harvest, and you shall not gather the grapes of your prohibited vines. It is a year of complete rest for the earth. [6]The fallow of the land will be food for you: for you, your manservant, your maidservant; your hired man and your resident who dwells with you; [7]for your livestock, and for the wild animals in your

---

cludes the covenant [26:45] that was mentioned in the *parasha* of *Mishpaṭim* [Exodus 24:7]. It appears here, out of order, to connect the laws of incest with the conditions under which the land was given, because incest was one of the things for which the land would vomit them out [18:28]. **[2]** The sabbatical years are the first condition listed (they are also discussed in the *parasha* of *Beḥuqqotai* [26:34*ff*]). **The land shall be given a rest** An Israelite must not allow a resident alien to sow his field on the Sabbatical year, just as we must not allow him to work on the Sabbath, as long as he is under our control. **the Sabbath of GOD** The Sabbatical year resembles the Sabbath day (this resemblance involves the mystery of the Days of Creation). **[3] its produce** "The land", mentioned in the previous verse, is the antecedent of the possessive pronoun. **[4] A Sabbath of Sabbath** explained above [16:31]. **[5]** It is well known that the word **accretion** is related to "add me on" [I Samuel 2:36] and that the word **your prohibited [vines]** is related to "Nazirite" [Numbers 6:2] [*cf. comment on* 15:31, 22:2]. **it is a year of complete rest** i.e., "...*because* it is a year of complete rest". In other words: You do not own the land during this year. **[6] The fallow of the land** denotes everything that the land yields spontaneously. **for you** [*plural*] for everybody. **for you** [*singular*] The owner has the same right as everyone else to eat the land's accretion. **[7]**

land. All of its produce will be to eat.

[8] Count yourselves seven weeks of years: seven years seven times. The time of your seven weeks of years will be forty-nine years. [9] You will sound the horn-cry in the seventh month, on the tenth of the month; on the Day of

---

your livestock denotes animals that you own, whereas **wild animals** denotes animals that you do not own.

[9] you will sound the horn Opinion is divided over whether the universe was created in Nisan or in Tishrey [Rosh Hashana 10b–11a]. We need not dwell on the topic, since the Exegetes have established [Rosh Hashana 27a] that we recite "This day, the anniversary of the first day of creation" in the Rosh HaShana prayer [*Musaf 'Amida* for Rosh HaShana]. Moreover, we see in the current verse that one blasts the horn of the jubilee year in Tishrey — namely, toward the beginning of the year. We also have the passage "Assemble the people..." [Deuteronomy 31:12] which tells us to read the Torah during the Sukkot festival. There the verse says "...that they may hear, and that they may learn" [Deuteronomy 31:12], and it is unlikely that this should take place after half of the year has elapsed. In addition, Scripture uses such phrases as "the harvest festival, at the end of the year" [Exodus 23:16] and "at the turn of the year" [Exodus 34:22]. The definitive proof, however, is the Sabbatical year, regarding which Scripture says, "Do not sow" [:11]. Now, the sowing season in the land of Israel begins in the month of Marḥeshvan. If the year were to begin in Nisan, then we could not harvest that which we planted in the sixth year. We could not plant on the following year (because it is the Sabbatical year), and since we could not harvest what was sown in the sixth year, it would be for all practical purposes as if we could not sow for two years in a row. Scripture, however, only tells us not to sow during the seventh year. ¶Yehuda HaParsi said that Israel used to follow a solar calendar. If this were true, then Moshe could not have taught us the exact length of a year, concerning

Atonement you will blast the horn throughout your land. [10]You will sanctify the fiftieth year and you will announce freedom in the land to all its inhabitants; a jubilee it is, and shall be, for you: you will return, everyone

---

which even today's astronomers have been unable to reach an agreement.[1] Not only do we rely on our tradition, but the very etymology of the word "month" also disproves HaParsi's thesis. The Sadducees [a derogatory reference to Karaites — Translator] claim that a "year" in our religion is a lunar year; but the term "year" does not even apply to the moon (just as the term "month" does not apply to the sun). Rather, by dividing the length of a month into the length of a year, people figured out that a year is approximately 12 months long. The remainder from this division was divided into the length of a lunar month, in order to calculate the fraction of a month left over, so that our months would be lunar months while our years would eventually conform to the solar year. Our Sages, of blessed memory, have accordingly transmitted to us a tradition, dating back to the times of Moshe, that the Sanhedrin must decree seven leap years in every 19-year cycle (even though the months themselves were proclaimed upon observing the new moon). The mysteries of the 19-year cycle can be derived from the science of astrology [*cf. comment on* Exodus 12:2]. **you** [*plural*] **will blast** The horn must be blown along all the highways. **[10] you will sanctify the fiftieth year** through the tilling of the soil, and through all its inhabitants. **freedom** This word means "liberty". Compare, "like a flying swallow" [Proverbs 26:2]. The term there denotes a bird which sings as long as it is free; but if it is forced into captivity, it will starve itself to death. **jubilee** [Hebrew: *yovel*] This word means "release". Our Sages, of

---

[1]The scholars of India add 12 minutes to 365¼ days. Ptolemy, on the other hand, and his colleagues, subtract 4 minutes and 48 seconds from 365¼ days. This amount is quite close to the solar year (but more recent scientists have proposed subtracting $\frac{1}{106}$ of a day, while others have proposed $\frac{1}{110}$, $\frac{1}{130}$, or $\frac{1}{180}$ of a day). These differences arise because the former astronomers calculate the sidereal year — from the moment when the sun is in conjunction with some star to the moment when the sun is next in conjunction with the same star. Other astronomers base their calculations on the angle of the ecliptic.

to his estate, and everyone will return to his family. [11]It is jubilee. It will be for you the fiftieth year. Do not sow, do not reap its accretion, and do not gather its forbidden grapes. [12]Since it is jubilee, it will be holy to you: You may eat of the field's produce. [13]In this jubilee year, everyone will return to his estate. [14]If you sell a commodity to your fellowman, or buy from the hand of your fellowman, you shall not defraud one another. [15]You shall buy from your fellowman according to the number of years after the jubilee; he will sell to you according to the number of years of crops. [16]For more years the price will increase, and for fewer years the price will decrease; for it is the number of crops that he sells you. [17]Do not defraud one another; fear your God. For I am GOD, your

---

blessed memory, have told us [Rosh HaShana 26a] that the word originally denoted a male lamb (as in, "trumpets of ram's horns [Hebrew: *yovlim*]" [Joshua 6:4]). The year was named after the horns that announce it. **for you** only for the Israelites. **everyone will return to his estate** In the jubilee year, as will be shortly explained, all sold land reverts to its original owners. **and everyone will return to his family** This applies to any servant who was sold to an Israelite. **[11] It is jubilee** and since it is the jubilee, **do not sow**. **[12] it will be holy to you** i.e., it is set apart from among the other years. **you may eat of the field** You all may eat the field's spontaneous produce, as it is written concerning the Sabbatical year [:6]. **[13] In this jubilee year** i.e., in the beginning of the year. **[14] buy** This word is a verbal noun. Scripture here employs brevity, instead of supplementing the infinitive with a verb in the indicative mood. The same construction appears in "Remember the Sabbath day" [Exodus 20:8] as well as in many other places. **If you** [*plural*] **sell** indicates that witnesses must participate. Similarly, **you** [*plural*] **shall not defraud** is addressed to the witnesses as well — **[15]** you must all terminate the contract after the appropriate number of years. **[16] the price will increase** The verb is the opposite of **decrease**. **[17]** The apparently redundant phrase **Do not defraud one another** serves to warn the seller. The original warn-

God. [18]Practice My statutes; observe My laws, and practice them; and you will dwell in the land securely. [19]The land will yield its produce, and you will eat to satisfaction; you will dwell securely upon it. [20]You may ask, 'What will we eat in the seventh year — we shall neither sow nor harvest our produce?' [21]I will order My blessing upon you in the sixth year, and it will yield produce for three years. [22]You will sow in the eighth year, and you will eat from the old produce — until the ninth year, until the arrival of its produce, you will eat of the old. [23]The land must not be sold into permanent ownership, for the

---

ing [:14] was addressed to the buyer. **I am GOD, your God** Since I am your God, I can exact punishment from the years of whomever defrauds his fellowman. However, **[18]** if you observe **My statutes**, then **[19]** the land will yield **its produce**. This reward is singled out, because Scripture is discussing the produce of the land. **[20]** The Sadducees [a derogatory reference to Karaites — Translator] claim that the word **our produce** proves that the year begins in Nisan. This proof is invalid, because here **our produce** almost certainly denotes what the land produces on its own. Should they assert that spontaneous yield is called "accretion" [:5], and not "produce", one can rebut them with "you may eat of the field's produce" [:12]. Besides, if they are correct, let them tell us how to treat the jubilee year. According to them, one may not then sow during the sixth year, nor during the seventh year, nor during the eighth year — we could begin to sow only at the end of the ninth year, and harvest it in the tenth year! If so, **[21]** then why does this verse mention only **three years**? The correct interpretation of **it will yield produce...**, in my opinion, is: I shall extend My blessing on the sixth year, that there will be not only enough for that year, but also enough for an additional year; and during the jubilee year, there will be enough for three years, but no more. The word **it will yield** is irregular, like "ministering to the king" [Hebrew: *mesharat*] [I Kings 1:15]. Of two consecutive *tav*'s, one is elided for the sake of euphony. **[22] old** [*masculine*] This word is the object of the preposition **from**, and here functions as a substantive. Compare, "from the ark-cover [*feminine*] you shall make the Cherubim

land is Mine: You are strangers and settlers in My midst. [24]In all the land in your possession, you will practice redemption of the land.

[25] If your fellowman becomes poor, and sells some of his inherited lands, his redeemer may come — a close relative — and redeem what his brother sold. [26]As for a man who has no redeemer: If he obtains sufficient means for redemption, [27]he will calculate the years of his sale, return the balance to the person to whom he sold it, and he will return to his holdings. [28] but if he cannot obtain sufficient means for reclaiming it to himself, his estate remains in the buyer's possession until the jubilee year. In the jubilee it shall go out, and return to his holdings.

[29]If a man sells a residential house in a walled city, its redemption shall be until the end of the year of its sale:

---

on its [*masculine*] two ends" [Exodus 25:19]. **[23] permanent ownership** From "GOD our God shall cut them off" [Psalms 94:23]. The *tav* is part of the triliteral root (as in "divorce" [Hebrew: *kritut*] [Deuteronomy 24:1]). The fundamental reason for these laws is that **the land is Mine**. Moshe himself said in his prayer, "GOD, you have been our dwelling place" [Psalms 90:1]. In other words: You are like an eternal dwelling place, into which "one generation passes away, and another generation comes" [Ecclesiastes 1:4]. **[24] the land of your possession** includes the Amorite lands as well as your inheritance in the land of Canaan.

[25] becomes poor This verb is an example of the so-called biliteral root; the middle consonant of the root has disappeared. It means "poor" or "impoverished". **close relative** i.e., closely related. **[27] calculate** a verb in the *pi'el* form. **[28] it shall go out** The abovementioned "estate" is the subject of the verb. Scripture employs metonymy, as in many other places, and uses a concrete noun to represent an attribute of the noun. Since Scripture goes on to

one year will be its redemption. [30] If it is not redeemed before the end of a full year, the house that is in a city that has a wall will remain the permanent possession of the buyer, throughout his generations; it will not revert at jubilee. [31] But houses in towns that have no surrounding wall will be considered with the open fields. It shall be redeemable, and revert at jubilee. [32] And as to the cities of the Levites — the houses of the cities of their possession — there will be eternal redemption for the Levites. [33] Whoever redeems from the Levites — the sale of a house, and a city of his holding, expires at the jubilee; for the houses of the cities of the Levites is their holding amid the Children of Israel. [34] The field of open land of their cities shall not be sold. It is their permanent hold-

---

discuss

[29] a residential house, we know that the passage "...and sells from his inheritance" [:25] refers to a field, or a vineyard. **a walled city** surrounded by a wall. **one year** [literally: days] The word denotes a year — until the days go through the cycle from cold to warm, summer and winter, returning to the way they were originally (with the sun in approximately the same location). We require the tradition ['Arakhin 31a] to define a complete year — whether it is a solar year, or a lunar year, or a lunar leap year. **[31] considered with** [literally: on] **the open fields** "On" here means "with", as in "the men came with [literally: on] the women" [Exodus 35:22]. **it** [*singular*] **shall be redeemable** i.e, each and every house may be redeemed (compare, "branches [*plural*] that run [*singular*] over the wall" [Genesis 49:22] and "...for her children [*plural*], because he [*singular*] is not" [Jeremiah 31:14]). **[32] eternal redemption** i.e., permanent redemption. After mentioning the permanent right of redemption, Scripture uses the same word when it says **[33] whoever redeems from the Levites**; but here the word simply means "to buy" (others say that the choice of words teaches us that the house may be redeemed even from a Levite buyer). The *vav* in **expires** is like the *f* of Arabic. The same laws apply to a

ing.

[35]If your brother grows poor, and if his fortune drops with you, you must support him. If a foreign resident, he will live with you. [36]Take no interest or usury from him; fear your God. Your brother will live with you. [37]Do not give him your money for interest, nor give him your food for usury. [38]I am GOD, your God, Who took you out of the land of Egypt; to give you the land of Canaan, to be your God.

[39]When your fellow man becomes poor with you, and is

---

single **house** as to an entire **city**.

[35] his fortune drops From "He shall not waver" [Psalms 112:6]. The *mem* is part of the triliteral root. Compare, "when I said, 'my foot slips'" [Psalms 94:18]. **your brother** i.e., an Israelite. **with you** You are obligated to help when he is with you, and when you are aware of him. **you must support him** This metaphor is the opposite of **his fortune drops**: you must keep him from falling. **a foreign resident** The above commandment applies to your own countryman; but even if he is a foreign resident, **he will live** with you (the verb is in the future tense). **[36] interest or usury** The Oral Tradition defines these terms precisely [Bava Meṣi'a 60b], and Scripture elaborates their meaning in the following verse. **Usury**, from "excessive" [e.g., Genesis 13:6], stems from a *lamed-heh* verb. The *tav* is extraneous, as in "deceit" [Zephaniah 3:13] and "perfect hatred" [Psalms 139:22]. **[37]** The *mem* in **usury** is also extraneous, like the *mem* in "ornament" [Leviticus 26:1]. **[38]** Scripture now says **I am GOD, your God, Who took you out of the land of Egypt** as if to say, "you were foreigners, and now I have given you an inheritance". This concept is related to "if a foreign resident, he will live with you" [:35] as well as to the previous passage, which discusses land redemption. Moreover, the entire passage of "if his fortune drops..." [:35] appears where it does on account of the law that if an Israelite in great need sells himself as a slave, he must go free at the Jubilee. Thus, all of the passages in

sold to you, do not make him do the work of a slave. [40]He will be with you like a hired man or a resident. He will serve with you until the jubilee; [41]then he will leave you, he and his children with him. He will return to his family, and he will return to his ancestral holdings. [42]For they are My servants, whom I took out of the land of Egypt. They will not be sold as one sells a slave. [43]Do not oppress him with hard labor. Fear your God. [44]The bondmen and bondmen that you will have — from the nations around you, from them you may purchase bondman and bondmaid; [45]and also from the children of the settlers who live among you — from them you may buy, and from their families among you which they will bear in your land. They will be part of your estate. [46]You will bequeath them to your children after you, to inherit the

---

this section are interrelated.

[39] is sold to you whether he sold himself, or whether he stole something from you and was sold by the Court. **[40] he will serve with you until the jubilee ... [41] then he will leave you, he and his children** The Sages have transmitted the tradition [Qiddushin 21b] that these verses apply to the slave of whom it was said "he shall serve him forever" [Exodus 21:6]. **[42] they are My servants** because I acquired them from the slavehouse. **[43] hard labor** This word should be rendered along the lines of the Aramaic translation. **[44] from the nations around you** e.g., 'Ammon, Mo'av, 'Edom, and 'Aram. **[45] and also from the children of the settlers** who now live in your land (the land of Canaan), but who were originally from the abovementioned nations, or Egypt, or any nation except the Seven Nations. Regarding the latter Scripture says, "you must not spare any soul" [Deuteronomy 20:16]. Since it is forbidden even to feed them, it is almost certain that when our Sages, of blessed memory, use the term "Canaanite slave" [Qiddushin 22b] they meant someone who lives in the land of Canaan but who is not of Canaanite lineage. On the other hand, possibly they knew the true meaning of these verses to be other than their literal

estate. You will always hold them in service. But your brothers, the children of Israel — do not oppress one another with hard labor.

[47] If an alien resident among you obtains means, and with him your brother becomes poor, and is sold to the alien resident among you, or to a transplanted alien family:
[48] After he is sold, he must have redemption; one of his brothers will redeem him. [49] Or his uncle or his cousin will redeem him, or some other relative in his family will redeem him. Or he may obtain the means, and be redeemed. [50] He will calculate with his buyer from the year when he was sold to him, until the year of the jubilee. The money for his sale will be according to the number of years: he will have been with him like the years of a hired servant. [51] If there are still many years, he will accord-

---

meaning — for our understanding is feeble compared to theirs. **[46] bequeath** a *hitpa'el* verb with a transitive sense, like "you shall draw" [Numbers 34:10]. **you will always hold them in service** i.e., it is *permissible*. Our Sages, however, of blessed memory, have told us [Giṭṭin 38b] that it is *obligatory*; and we accept what they say. **but your brothers, the children of Israel** You should distinguish between your brother and a foreigner.

[47] transplanted that is, "rooted" — someone of Gentile ancestry who has adopted the religion of Israel. This word has no cognate, but it is the opposite of "uproot you" [Psalms 52:7]. See also "you shall hamstring their horses" [Joshua 11:6]. **[49] or he may obtain the means** He could find a lost object, or he could inherit property from a dead relative. Nevertheless, Scripture first speaks of his brother and his family, because that is the more usual case. **[50] his buyer** This word, with a *heh*, means the same as it does without a *heh*. **when he was sold** a verbal noun in the *nif'al* form. The years when he was with his buyer are considered **like the years of a hired servant**. **[51] he will accordingly repay the**

ingly repay the redemption, from the money of his sale. [52]If there are few years remaining till the year of jubilee, he will calculate accordingly. He will repay his redemption according to his years. [53]He shall be to him like an annual workhand. He must not oppress him with hard labor, in your sight. [54]If he is not thereby redeemed, he will leave in the year of jubilee, he and his children with him. [55]For the Children of Israel are servants to Me; they are My servants, whom I took out of the land of Egypt. I am GOD, your God. [26:1]Do not make idols for yourselves, do not place a graven image or a monument for yourselves. Do not place in your land a stone ornament for prostration, for I am GOD, your God.

---

redemption [money] He will calculate for him the appropriate proportion of the original purchase price. **if there are still many years** whether the remaining years are many or few ...". The *vav* connecting these two clauses is like the Arabic *f.* **[53]** Scripture repeats **like an annual workhand** in order to add **he will not oppress him with hard labor, in your sight**. This means that we may not allow a foreigner to oppress him with hard labor. **[54] If he is not thereby redeemed** "Thereby" denotes the years remaining until the Jubilee (some say that it denotes the abovementioned redeemers [:48-49]). **[55]** The current use of the phrase **the children of Israel are My servants** [*cf.* :42] is addressed to the foreigner who buys an Israeli slave. **[26:1] monument** for the abovementioned **graven image** (the meaning of which is known). **ornament** a noun, like the word "usury" [25:37]. It denotes a painted stone, from "they have more than the heart can describe" [Psalms 73:7] and "delightful craftsmanship" [Isaiah 2:16]. **do not place in your land** which is how Mercury was generally worshiped [Sanhedrin 60b]. **for I am GOD, your God** and it is I to whom you must prostrate yourselves (as it is rendered in the Aramaic translation of Jerusalem [no such translation is known – Translator]). ¶**do not make idols for yourselves** Scripture has repeated its admonition against idolatry, since one might be sold to a Gentile. One may not service one's mas-

[2]You shall observe My Sabbaths, and you shall revere My sanctuary. I am GOD.

[3]If you follow my laws, and observe My commandments, and practice them, [4]I will provide your rains in their season; the land will yield its produce, and the tree of the field will yield its fruit. [5]Threshing will last you until vintage, and vintage will extend until planting. You will

---

ters' idol, [2] nor may one serve one's masters on the Sabbath, though the foreigner may have bought him for that purpose. **revere My sanctuary** One must go to the Sanctuary on the three festivals. The sense of these verses is probably: Do not make idols for yourselves, since "they are My servants" (which was just stated prior to this); and since they are My servants, they must serve Me alone and no others. The injunction to **observe My sabbaths** also includes the Sabbatical years; while **revere My sanctuary** also denotes the jubilee year, as it is written, "it will be sanctified by you" [25:12]. In my opinion, "observe my sabbaths" is mentioned on account of having mentioned "to prostrate yourselves upon it" [:1], along the lines of "every Sabbath, all flesh shall come to bow to the ground before me" [Isaiah 66:23]. In other words: You must come every Sabbath to prostrate yourselves before Me — not on some ornamental stone, but only in My sanctuary. Thus, Scripture mentions the choice day (which was chosen for the service of GOD, as I have explained [*comment on* Genesis 2:3]), as well as the choice place. **I am GOD** Who rested from all labor on the Sabbath, and Whose Glory resides in the Sanctuary, and for Whose sake **you shall revere**.

[3] **If you follow My laws ... observe, and practice ...** We are required to *study* and to *teach* as well as to *do*. [4] The *vav* in **I will provide** is like the *vav* in "the earth was formless and empty" [Genesis 1:2]. ¶A verb with a *vav* that is accented on the ultima is always in the future tense; if it is accented on the penultimate it is in the past tense, with very few exceptions. **its produce** from "the mountains bring him food" [Job 40:20]. It is not known whether the *yod* is part of the triliteral root, or whether, like the word "liv-

eat your bread to satiety, and you will dwell securely in your land. [6] I will provide peace in the land; you will rest and none will frighten you. I will exterminate evil animals from the land, and the sword will not pass through your land. [7] You will pursue your enemies, and they will fall before you by the sword. [8] Five of you will pursue a hundred; a hundred of you will pursue ten thousand. Your enemies will fall before you by the sword. [9] I shall turn to you, and make you fruitful, and increase you. I

---

ing creature" [*cf.* Genesis 7:4], it is not part of the triliteral root. [5] The phrase **threshing will last until vintage** indicates that the phrase "when you gather your products from the field" [Exodus 23:16] applies to the vineyard as well. **to satiety** a verbal noun. The word **securely**, like the word "alone" [Numbers 23:9], means the same thing both with and without a *lamed.* Scripture mentions satiety before security because it is fundamental. **you shall dwell in security** for in times of famine, people wander from their homes (compare, "it will not henceforth yield its produce for you; a fugitive and a wanderer will you be" [Genesis 4:12]). [6] **I will provide peace in the land** among yourselves **and none will frighten you** neither wild beast nor enemy; rather, [7] you will pursue the enemy, and he will fall before you. The wonder will be that [8] a small number of you will pursue a large number of enemies. I have already explained in *Sefer Moznayyim* that the words "ten", "hundred", "thousand", and "myriad" (ten thousands) are approximate quantities. It is customary to exaggerate numbers by multiplying them by ten, as in "now you are worth all ten thousand of us" [II Samuel 18:3]. Here Scripture exceeds this custom — five people pursuing one hundred people involves twice the usual proportion. Moreover, each of a hundred people will himself be able to pursue a hundred people.[1] Scripture repeats **your enemies will fall** to convey that they will fall one after another, and not get up.

---

[1]Certain people offer the explanation that when individuals are united, each can pursue a greater number. They apply this explanation to the verse "how could one chase a thousand..." [Deuteronomy 32:30]. But there is no need to take things so literally.

will fulfill My covenant with you. [10]You will eat from the old, aged harvest. You will clear out the old because of the new. [11]I will place My Habitation in your midst, and shall not loathe you. [12]I shall go about in your midst. I shall be your God, and you will be My nation. [13]I am GOD, your God, Who brought you out of the land of Egypt, from being their slaves; I broke the traces of your yoke, and led you out upright.

[14]But if you will not obey Me, and will not practice all

---

[9] **I shall turn to you** i.e., by increasing your wealth; and also by making you fruitful, and by increasing you with sons and daughters. In my opinion, the word **I shall make you fruitful** is the opposite of "the barren womb" [Proverbs 30:16]. **I will fulfill My covenant with you** that you be "as many as the stars in heaven" [Deuteronomy 1:10] and "as the dust of the earth" [Genesis 13:16]. [10] **you will eat from the old, aged harvest** The wonder will be – despite your great numbers – that whoever wants to will be able to eat **old** produce, or produce **aged** even further than the old produce (the word is in the *nif'al* form). Some people will have to take the old crop out of their houses before the new crop, because there will no room to store it (one commentator has said that **you will clear out** denotes taking it out into the field). [11] **I will place my Habitation** Do not fear that you will ever come to lack, for My Glory will dwell with you, and I am not like a person who loathes always to remain in the same place. Also, when you travel to the land of your enemies, even if the Sanctuary is not among you, [12] My Glory will walk amid you. Thus, I will be **God** to you, and you will be My nation; [13] and it is for this reason that **I brought you out of the land of Egypt**. **the traces of your yoke** Scripture compares Israel to a plowing bull who works his master's land. Israel, in fact, was enslaved through the building of the land (for so it is written [Exodus 1:11]). **upright** bearing an erect posture.

[14] Certain empty-headed people have said that the curses are more numerous than the blessings. This is untrue. Rather, the blessings are given in general terms, whereas the curses are given

these commandments, [15] and if you reject My decrees and if you loathe My precepts, not to practice all My commandments, through your nullifying My covenant: [16] I will also act like this to you. I shall command upon you confusion, the *shaḥefet*, and the *qaddaḥat*: destroying the eyes, and which distress the soul. You will sow your seed in vain, for your enemies will eat it. [17] I will turn My anger against you, and you will be defeated before your enemies. Your foes will dominate you, and you will flee when no one pursues you. [18] If after these you will not obey Me, I will continue to punish you seven times above

---

in detail in order to impress and to frighten the listeners. If you read carefully, what I have said will become evident. **all the commandments** the ones mentioned above. **[15] nullifying** This is an irregular word. Verbal nouns often deviate from the normal construction. **[16] I shall command upon you** like a man in command of another, who can have his will with him. **confusion, the *shaḥefet*, and the *qaddaḥat*** These are known illnesses. The connecting preposition here has the sense of "with". **Confusion** means, you will be confused and will not know what to do (although some say that **confusion** means "suddenly"). Many people have drawn the conclusion, without cause, that ***shaḥefet*** and ***qaddaḥat*** are both plant diseases (similar to "blasting" and "mildew", as it is written [Amos 4:9]), on account of the phrase **you will sow in vain**. The actual meaning is that they will contract illnesses; then, when enemies come to their villages and eat their grain, no one will be able to go out against them and drive them away. **destroying the eyes...** These illnesses will darken the eyes and distress the soul. The phrase **distress the soul**, like the phrase "a liar gives ear..." [Proverbs 17:4], is missing an *'alef*. Some people say that the word **eyes** represents the entire body, because it is followed by the contrasting phrase **which distress the soul**; but this interpretation is groundless. **[17] I will turn My anger** [literally: My face] this means, My wrath, My anger (as in "her ill disposition [literally: her face] was no longer with her" [I Samuel 1:18]). Those who survive the diseases will be defeated if they go out in battle against their enemies. They will even flee when no one pur-

your sins: [19]I will destroy the pride of your strength. I will make your skies like iron, and your land like copper. [20]Your efforts will go to waste, for your land will not yield its produce, nor will the tree of the land yield its fruit. [21] If you will walk against Me in stubbornness, and will not consent to obey Me — I will continue the plague against you, seven times corresponding to your sins: [22]I will send upon you the wild animal, which will bereave

---

sues them, in the way of the Aramean camp [II Kings 7:7]. **[18] if after these** i.e., if after these catastrophes. **seven** a round number, often used simply to denote "many" (as in, "a just man falls seven times, and yet rises up again" [Proverbs 24:16] and "the barren has born seven" [I Samuel 2:5]). Scripture does not imply that God will return sevenfold **for your sins**; rather, He will **continue** with yet another punishment (as in, "a mighty voice, that has not continued" [Deuteronomy 5:19]). **above your sins** i.e., because of your sins. Some people incorrectly say that the number **seven** **[19]** is to be taken literally. If we consider **I will destroy** to be One; **your skies like iron**, Two; **your land like copper**, "will go to waste" [:20], the produce of the land, and the fruit of the trees — we have only six. We would need to add the plague of "wild animal" [:22] to obtain a total of seven. **the pride of your strength** prosperity (as in, "Yeshurun grew fat" [Deuteronomy 32:15]). Pride, once it is shattered, plummets into humiliation. **[20] Your efforts will go to waste** whereby you toiled in working the land. **[21] stubbornness** Although this word has no cognate, many people agree that it denotes boldness, contention, strengthening of resolve and dismissal of fear, so as not to be vanquished. Others relate the word to "all that had happened" [Genesis 42:29]. They interpret the word along the lines of the Philistines' statement, "It is not His hand that smote us: it was a happenstance" [I Samuel 6:9]. Both explanations either require an implied "with" (as in "[within] six days" [Exodus 20:11]), or else the sentence means, "if you walk [the ways of] stubbornness against me". I have shown you many similar sentences. Note that Scripture here says **corresponding to your sins** — which means that He will not exceed their magnitude — whereas the previous phrase "above your sins" [:18] modified

you, destroy your livestock, and diminish your numbers. Your roads will become desolate. [23] If through these you will not subject yourselves to Me, and you walk against Me in stubbornness, [24] Even I will walk against you in stubbornness. I will smite you also, seven times upon your sins. [25] I will bring the sword upon you, exacting retribution for the covenant, and you will gather within your cities; but I will send pestilence among you and you will be given into the enemy's hands. [26] When I break your bread supply, ten women will bake your bread in one oven, and will divide your bread by weight. You will eat

---

"to punish you" [:18] and means "*because of* your sins". **[22] I will send upon you** compare, "I will send upon you" [Exodus 8:17]. **bereave you** through the killing of children **diminish your numbers** through the killing of adults **your roads will become desolate** for no way will be free from the fear of wild animals (i.e., animals unowned by any man, as I have explained [*comment on* 25:7]). **[23] you will not subject yourselves** The future tense of a *nif'al* verb. **[24] upon your sins** This phrase modifies the verb **I will smite you** [and not the adverb "sevenfold"; *cf. comments on* :18, :21]. **[25] retribution for the covenant** Concerning this, I have already said [*comment on* 25:1] that the covenant herein mentioned was the one ratified at Sinai and mentioned in the *parasha* of *Mishpaṭim.* When Israel accepted it upon themselves, saying, "we will do, and we will obey" [Exodus 24:7] the covenant was then ratified, and all of this *parasha* was given. **you will gather within your cities** on account of the sword; but I will send epidemics and famine there, until you will want to be captured by the enemy — that is, **you will be** voluntarily **given into the enemy's hands** (the verb is in the *nif'al* form). **[26] When I break your bread supply** The verb is in the infinitive form, vocalized with a *ḥiriq* as in "when she lay down, or when she arose" [Genesis 19:33]. Scripture uses the verb "to break" because "supply" is here figuratively called a "staff". Similarly, Isaiah speaks of "the support of bread" [Isaiah 3:1] because "bread strengthens man's heart" [Psalms 104:15]. **ten women** a round number. It was the custom in Israel

and not be satisfied.

[27]If through this you will not listen to Me, but will walk against Me in stubbornness, [28]I will walk against you with the fury of stubbornness, and I will punish you seven times upon your sins. [29]You will eat the flesh of your sons, and the flesh of your daughters you will eat. [30]I will destroy your altars, and I will shatter your sun-temples. I will cast your corpses upon the corpses of your idols. I will loathe you. [31]I will reduce your cities to rubble; I will desolate your sanctuaries; I will not smell the

---

for every household to bake in its own oven enough bread for the week. The arrangement of loaves on the Sabbath [24:8] provides evidence for this practice. **will divide your bread by weight** because it will be so meager. **you will eat and not be satisfied** Hunger normally abates after one has eaten a little, but you will not be satisfied even with great amounts of food.

[27] **if through this** i.e., if through this calamity (similarly, "if through these" [:23] means, "if through these calamities" — the ones that have been mentioned). [28] The phrase **upon your sins** modifies the verb **I will punish you** [*cf. comment on* :24]. [29] **you will eat the flesh of your sons and the flesh of your daughters** This is the most extreme stage of a famine. [30] You will have no place to cry out and to pray for deliverance from the famine, for I shall destroy **your altars** (the places where you offer your sacrifices). **sun-temples** houses built for sun-worship, from "sun" [Job 30:28]. The *nun* is extraneous, like the *nun* in "compassionate women" [Lamentations 4:10]. **your corpses** i.e., your bodies, as in "a trampled carcass" [Isaiah 14:19]. "Idols" is a derogatory term for idol-worship, from "as one removes dung" [I Kings 14:10]. The sense of the verse is: You will be killed as you gather together in the houses of idol worship; your enemies will destroy the images of your useless idols, while I shall not save you. **I will loathe you** This means either that the Divine Presence will depart, or that [31] **your cities** will be devastated and your sanctuaries — which were once My sanctuaries — will be destroyed. **I will not smell the odor**

odor of your offerings. [32]I will desolate the land so that your enemies who occupy it will be astounded by it. [33]I will scatter you among the nations, and I will draw the sword after you. Your land will be desolate, and your cities will be rubble, [34]then the land will appease its Sabbaths all the days of its desolation and your stay in your enemies' land. Then will the land rest, and expiate its Sabbaths. [35]It will rest all the days of its desolation, in that it did not rest during your Sabbaths, while you dwelt upon it. [36]I will bring faintness of their heart to those of you who survive in the land of their enemies. The sound of rustling leaves will chase them; they will flee as one

---

of your offerings Although GOD's Glory fills the heavens and the earth, Scripture here speaks metaphorically and means, "I will no longer accept your burnt offerings". Similarly, concerning Noah Scripture says, "GOD smelled the pleasing odor" [Genesis 8:21]. After mentioning **your cities** and **your sanctuaries**, **[32]** Scripture proceeds to mention **the land** – i.e., the entire land of Israel. **will be astounded by it** The destruction will be so vast that it will astound even the occupying enemies (the opposite of "...the rejoicing of the whole earth" [Lamentations 2:15]). **[33] I will scatter** a verb in the *pi'el* form. Not only will you be scattered, but I will also draw the sword against you. **I will draw** [Hebrew: I will empty] from its sheath. **your land will be desolate** This phrase is connected to the subsequent verse, so as to read, "*When* your **land** will be **desolate**, *then* **[34] the land will appease...**" (the latter verb means "repay", as in "as a hireling, he shall fulfill his day" [Job 14:6] and "her iniquity has been repayed" [Isaiah 40:2]). **its Sabbaths** the Sabbatical and the jubilee years. Compare, "until the land has made good her Sabbaths" [II Chronicles 36:21], as I have there explained. **its desolation** a noun. The formation of nouns is often irregular. **all the days of its desolation, and your stay in your enemies' land** When the land is desolate of you it will rest, and find respite, to make up for its Sabbatical years. **[35] it will rest all the days of its desolation** it will rest an amount of time equivalent to the number of years owed, as explained in Ezekiel [Ezekiel 4:5–6].

flees the sword, and fall, when no one pursues. [37]They
will stumble upon one another, as before the sword,
without a pursuer. You will have no standing before your
enemies. [38]You will be lost among the nations; the land
of your enemies will consume you. [39]The survivors
among you will weaken for their sins in their enemies'
lands; they will even weaken for the sins of their fathers
among them. [40]They will confess their sin, and the sin of
their fathers, in their faithlessness, in being faithless to
Me — that they even trespassed against Me with stubbornness. [41]So I walk against them with stubbornness,
and bring them into their enemies' land. Then their uncircumsized heart will capitulate, and then they shall

---

[36] Scripture mentions **those of you who survive** because it previously said "I will draw the sword against you" [:33]. **faintness** an *'ayin-'ayin* verb (like "lifting up their hands" [Nehemiah 8:6]), from "fainthearted" [Deuteronomy 20:8]. The will be so afraid that **the sound of rustling leaves** will put them to flight. **rustling** an adjective, from a verb in the *nif'al* form. The *nun* of the triliteral root is absorbed. [37] **one another** [literally: each upon his brother] each upon his friend. **standing** The presence of the *tav* indicates that this is the *hif'il* form of an *'ayin-vav* verb, like "donation" [Exodus 25:2]. [38] **will consume you** Whenever people are exiled to another place, where the air and the water are different, they normally die in great numbers. [39] **the survivers** i.e., some among the survivers. **will weaken** an *'ayin-'ayin* verb (like "turned" [Ezekiel 1:9]), from "his flesh shall consume away" [Zechariah 14:12] and "there shall be a stench" [Isaiah 3:24]. **they will even weaken for the sins of their fathers among them** compare, "our fathers have sinned" [Lamentations 5:7], as I have explained in the Book of Lamentations. [40] **they will confess** a verb in the *hitpa'el* form. Although **their fathers** committed **their faithlessness, in being faithless to Me**; it was the sons themselves who **even trespassed against Me** and acted **with stubbornness.** [41] **Even I...** i.e., So have I done with them: I have punished them by bringing them into **their enemies'** land, until **their uncircumsized**

repay their sin. [42]I will recall my covenant of Ya'aqov, as well as my covenant of Yiṣḥaq, as well as my covenant with Avraham I will recall; and I will recall the land. [43]The land will be forsaken without them, and it will appease its Sabbaths in its desolation from them, and they shall repay their sin, because and because they have rejected My precepts and they have loathed My decrees. [44]Even although this — their being in their enemies' land — I will not reject them, nor loath them, to annihilate them, to break My covenant with them. For I am GOD, their God. [45]I will remember of them the original

---

heart capitulated, as I shall further explain. They shall **repay their sin** means, they shall make restitution, they will be punished for it [*cf. comment on* :34]. **[42] I will recall My covenant** The object of the verb is also connected to the phrase that follows it, in the sense of, "My covenant, the covenant of Ya'aqov". Compare, "the prophesy that was the prophesy of 'Oded the prophet" (literally, "the prophesy 'Oded the prophet") [II Chronicles 15:8] and "your chiefs, the chiefs of your tribes" (literally, "your chiefs of your tribes") [Deuteronomy 29:9]. Sa'adya Gaon said that Scripture begins first with Ya'aqov, because he was party to the covenant all of his life. **[43] the land will be forsaken without them** i.e., I will recall the land, which has made restitution for its Sabbaths, and which was forsaken without them; and I will also recall that they have repaid **their sin. because and because** The first corresponds to **they have rejected My precepts** while the second corresponds to **they have loathed My decrees**. The *bet* is extraneous, like the *bet* of "at first" [Genesis 13:4]. **[44] even although** A stylistic embellishment, since one adverb would have sufficed. Similar constructions appear throughout Scripture, like "only but with Moses" [Numbers 12:2] and "for want of no graves" [Exodus 14:11]. **I will not reject them ... to annihilate them** only to punish them, until their hearts will capitulate [*cf.* :41]. **loathe them** turn away from them, or abhor them. **to break My covenant** which I have sworn to them — even though *they* have broken My covenant, as it is written [:15] — I shall not break My covenant with them, for I

covenant, of which I brought them out of the land of Egypt in sight of the nations, to be for them a God. I am Hashem" [46]These are the decrees and the precepts and the teachings which GOD gave, between Him and the children of Israel, on Mount Sinai, through Moshe.

[27:1]GOD told Moshe: [2]Speak to the Children of Israel, and say to them: "If a man expresses a vow with the

---

am God. **[45] I will** forever **remember of them the original covenant** i.e., the covenant that was ratified at Sinai. The people there are called the **original** generation, as opposed to the descendents who were exiled to the land of their enemies (some say that the term denotes the forefathers; in that case, **which I brought out** must perforce mean, "those of whom I swore to their forefathers that I would bring their children out of slavery" — but the former interpretation, in my opinion, is correct). **[46] These are the decrees and the precepts** The ones that are written in the *parashiyyot* of *Yitro* and *Mishpaṭim* as well as in the *parasha* of *Behar.* **which GOD gave, between Him and the children of Israel** This alludes to the covenant at Mount Sinai, since Moshe ceased ascending Mount Sinai once the Sanctuary was made and the Glory entered the Tent of Assembly. For the same reason, Scripture now mentions

[27:1] the passage of valuations — on account of its having been said on Mount Sinai (for so it is written at the end [:34]) — unlike the next book, which begins with "GOD spoke to Moshe in the wilderness of Sinai, in the Tent of Assembly" [Numbers 1:1] like the beginning of the book of *Vayyiqra.* **[2] expresses** i.e., specifies, makes clear. **the valuation of animate things** This involves a case where someone takes a vow, saying, "If GOD will do such-and-such for me, I will redeem my soul with its valuation" (or his son's valuation, or the valuation of an animal, etc). ¶All the grammarians agree that the *khaf* is extraneous, and that the word means "valuation". One opinion, however, holds that the *khaf* indicates the second person masculine singular possessive and denotes the kohen. "As the valuation of the kohen" [:12] would then be explained to read, "as your valuation, of you", and the *heh*

valuation of animate things to GOD: [3] The valuation of the male from twenty years of age to sixty years of age — the valuation is fifty silver shekels of the holy shekels; [4] if it is a female, the valuation is thirty shekels. [5] If from five years of age to twenty years of age — the valuation of the male is twenty shekels; for the female, ten

---

would be classified as a vocative *heh.* Similarly, "the valuation" [:23] must perforce be an irregular word, like "within my tent" [literally: within the my tent] [Joshua 7:21]. In my opinion, however, the latter word means, "the tent, which was my tent". The same argument can apply to "the your valuation". **animate** which includes both people and animals. **[3] from twenty years** beginning with the age when one enters into the census. **sixty** when one becomes old. The opinion of many is that these laws are simply unexplained decrees. Thus **[5]** from the age of one month until the age of five years, one must give five *sheqalim* — even for someone only one day older than one month, one must give five *sheqalim.* Sa'adya Gaon believed, however, that one must give one *sheqel* for every year of age, up till and including the age of five. Nevertheless, the majority opinion is that there are four fixed valuations (corresponding to the four stages of a person's life). The second stage extends up to and including the age of nineteen, and the third stage extends up to and including the age of fifty-nine. Within each of these stages, one's valuation always remains at the same level it assumed at the beginning of the stage. The fourth stage lasts roughly fifteen years, giving a total of seventy-five years for the four stages of life. ¶The truth is that one passes from each stage to the next at the exact number of years specified ['Arakhin 18a]. One might entertain the supposition, however, that the passing of a single day in a year is as good as the passing of a year [e.g., Rosh HaShana 2b]. We need not depend on the tradition alone to refute this idea — we can simply point out, Why would it then be necessary to specify a lower limit of one month in the one month to five year interval? ¶The period until five years, and the period until twenty years, might lead one to conclude that a man's valuation goes up one *sheqel* every year until the age of sixty, at which point his valuation begins to decrease. One can answer the "one month" argument within the context of this supposition

shekels. [6]From the age of a month to the age of five years — the valuation of the male is five silver shekels; for the female the valuation is three silver shekels. [7]If from sixty years of age and upward — if a male, the valuation is fifteen shekels; for the female, ten shekels. [8]If he is too poor for the valuation, he will present him before the kohen, and the kohen will assess him. According to what the vower can afford the kohen will assess him.

[9]If it is a beast from which they may bring a sacrifice to

---

by stating simply that a person younger than one month has no valuation. However, what can one say about the period over sixty years? Does one continue to decrease the valuation *ad infinitum*? ¶Clearly, all of these alternate explanations are erroneous. The laws must be understood as Scriptural decrees. For this reason we cannot expect a consistent proportion between the valuation of a male and that of a female. After the age of sixty, the male valuation exceeds the female valuation by one-third; between the ages of five and twenty, the male exceeds the female by one half; from one month till five years, and also from twenty years to sixty years, the male exceeds the female by two-fifths. **[8] will assess** the person being assessed, and the one paying the assessment, are jointly evaluated. The word is related to "concerning You, there is no reckoning" [Psalms 40:6], but here it is in the *hif'il* form (as in **the kohen will assess him**), in order to differentiate its meaning from that of "he will arrange it before GOD" [24:8]. **he will present him** either

- "The kohen" is the subject of this verb, as if Scripture had said, "the kohen will present him before the kohen" (i.e., before himself). I have explained the phrase "he will pour some on the kohen's left palm" [14:15] along similar lines. This construction conforms to Hebrew usage.

or

- The person who vowed is the subject of the verb, and he presents himself before the kohen.

GOD, everything which he gives therefrom to GOD will be holy. [10]He must not exchange it, nor may he replace it: neither good with bad nor bad with good. If he does replace one beast with another beast, it and its replacement will be holy. [11]If it is any ritually impure beast, from which they may not bring a sacrifice to GOD, he will present the beast before the kohen. [12]The kohen will assess it, whether good or bad; as the valuation of the kohen, so shall it be. [13]If he redeems it, he will add a fifth to the valuation. [14]If a man dedicates his house to be holy to GOD, the kohen will assess it, whether good or bad; as the kohen assesses it, so it will be fixed. [15]If the dedicator redeems his house, he will add to it a fifth of the money of its valuation, and it will be his. [16]If a man dedicates from his hereditary land to GOD, the assessment will be according to its crop. A crop of a *ḥomer* of barley corresponds to fifty silver shekels. [17]If from the jubilee year he dedicates his field, it will be fixed at its valuation. [18] If he dedicates his field after the jubilee, the kohen will reckon the money for him according to the years remaining till the jubilee year, and subtracted from the valuation. [19] If the man who dedicates it redeems the land, he will add to it a fifth of its valuation, and it will become

---

[14] it will be fixed meaning, it will remain. **[16] from his hereditary land** within the territory that the nation of Israel has inherited. **a *ḥomer* of barley** Scripture states elsewhere [Ezekiel 45:11] that there are exactly ten *batim* in a *ḥomer*. In the same place, a *bat* is said to be equivalent to an *'efa*. Thus, land seeded with an *'efa* of barley would be valued at five *sheqalim*. This too is a decree of the King, concerning the wealth of His servant. **[17] if from the jubilee year** within the year itself. **[18] will be subtracted from the valuation** "The time that has passed since the jubilee" is

his. [20]If he does not redeem it, and if it was sold to another man, it may no longer be redeemed. [21]When the land goes out at jubilee, it will be holy to GOD, like a dedicated field; his estate will belong to the kohen. [22]If he dedicates land that he bought, which is not of his hereditary estate, to GOD, [23]the kohen will reckon for him the amount of the valuation until the year of the jubilee. He will pay the assessment on that day, holy to GOD. [24]In the jubilee year the land will return to the one from whom he bought it, to the one to whom it belongs as inherited land. [25]All valuations will be in holy shekels, twenty gerahs to the shekel. [26]However, a firstling beast, which is first-born to GOD — no man will dedicate it; whether it is an ox or a sheep, it belongs to GOD. [27]If of the ritually impure beast, it will be redeemed at the valuation, and he will add to it its fifth. If

---

the implied subject of the verb. [19] The *vav* in **if he redeems** here functions like the Arabic *f*. The verse is a continuation of the previous verses, since Scripture is primarily discussing valuation — in the case when the field is redeemed, and [20] in the case when the field is not redeemed. **and if it was sold** i.e., *or* if it was sold, the hereditary owner of the field may no longer redeem it. Once they sell it, it is consecrated to GOD. [21] **when it goes out at the jubilee** Scripture now mentions that the field leaves its buyer at the jubilee, the same as any other field. **like a dedicated field** When someone vows to consecrate his field, it also goes to the kohen. Here, in addition, the monetary valuation of the property goes **to the kohen** — that is, to the one who made the original valuation (he need *not* be the High Priest). [23] **the amount** as in "the number of persons" [Exodus 12:4]. [24] **the one from whom he bought it** this is the original seller, as Scripture subsequently explains: **to the one to whom it belongs as hereditary land.** [26] **consecrated as a first-offering** It is already known that it belongs to GOD (the verb is in the passive mood). This verse discusses the case when someone declares, "I will donate this first-born to

it is not redeemed, it will be sold at valuation. [28]However, anything dedicated, which a man may dedicate to GOD from anything that is his — from a person, or a beast, or from a field of his estate — will not be sold or redeemed. Anything dedicated is most holy to GOD. [29]The ban of any person, who will be banned, will not be ransomed. He will be put to death. [30]Every tithe of the land — from the grain of the land, from the fruit of the tree — belongs to GOD, is holy to GOD. [31]If a man does redeem a part of his tithe, he will add its fifth to it. [32]Every tithe of cattle, or of the flock — everything that passes under the rod: The tenth will be consecrated to GOD. [33]He must not discriminate between good and bad, nor will he replace it. If he does replace it, it and its replacement will be holy. It cannot be redeemed." [34]These are the commandments that GOD commanded Moshe to the Children

---

GOD". [27] **if** the abovementioned first-born is **of** a **ritually inpure beast, it will be redeemed at the valuation** plus an additional one-fifth, since he consecrated it. He may alternatively give a lamb (for so it is written [Exodus 13:12–13]), if he does not consecrate it, or if it was sold. In the case of a firstling donkey [Exodus 13:13], he must give the valuation, *and* a lamb, although many people disagree [the *halakha*, in fact, is that a firstling donkey can be redeemed either with a lamb, or with money [Bekhorot 11a] — Translator]. [28] **from anything that is his** i.e., anything under his control. **a person** compare, "I will consecrate their cities" [Numbers 21:2]. [29] The verb **will be banned** is in the passive mood, like "will be stood up alive" [16:10]. [32] **under the rod** the shepherd's rod. The animals selected for GOD are: 1) the first-born, and 2) every tenth animal. The two categories have equal status, except that the latter, unlike the firstborn, can be redeemed. Thus, a man must donate his firstborn, as well as one-tenth of his livestock — just as he must donate his firstfruits [Exodus 23:19] and a tithe [Deuteronomy 14:22] of all edible vegetable products. [33] **discriminate** meaning, "distinguish". I have already explained [*comment on*

of Israel, on Mount Sinai.

Genesis 1:5] that this word is related to "morning". [34] I have already explained **on Mount Sinai** earlier in this *parasha* [*comment on* 26:46]. Whoever has a mind to understand the mysteries of the universe, will grasp the inner meaning of the first-born, and of the tithes [*cf. comment on* Exodus 20:14]. Abraham practiced tithe-giving [Genesis 14:20] as did our father Ya'aqov, may he rest in peace [Genesis 28:22]. I shall reveal somewhat more of this mystery when I discuss the Second Tithe [*comment on* Deuteronomy 14:22], with the help of the One to Whom there is no second.

1 solar year $\approx$ 365 days, 5 hours, 48 minutes, and 46 seconds
= 31,556,926 seconds.

$365\frac{1}{4}$ days $- \frac{1}{128}$ days = 31,556,925 seconds.

1 Gregorian year = $365\frac{1}{4}$ days $- \frac{3}{400}$ days
= 31,556,952 seconds.

1 sidereal year $\approx$ 365 days, 6 hours, 9 minutes, and 10 seconds
= 31,558,150 seconds.

1 synodic month $\approx$ 29 days, 12 hours, 44 minutes, and 2.78 seconds
= 2,551,442.78 seconds.

1 Jewish month = 29 days, 12 hours, 44 minutes, and $3^1/_3$ seconds.

1 sidereal month $\approx$ 27 days, 7 hours, 43 minutes, and 11 seconds
= 2,360,591 seconds.

1 19-year cycle = 12 12-month years + 7 13-month years
= 235 Jewish months
= 599,589,183 $^1/_3$ seconds.

1 mean Jewish year = $\frac{1}{19}$ of a 19-year cycle
$\approx$ 31,557,325 seconds
= 365 days, 5 hours, 55 minutes, and 25 seconds.

Citation Index

Index of Talmudic References

All references are to the Babylonian Talmud unless otherwise stated